Fire In The Corporate Belly

Renewing the Company
Body, Soul & Bottom Line

Tom FitzGerald

Fire in The Corporate Belly
ISBN 1-882195-06-4

Copyright ©2004 by FitzGerald Associates

FitzGerald Associates
P.O. Box 27
Lake Forest, Illinois 60045
www.ManagementConsultants.com

Library of Congress Cataloguing in Publication Data

FitzGerald, Tom.
Fire in the corporate belly: renewing the company body, soul
& bottom line / Tom FitzGerald
ISBN 1-882195-06-4
1. Business Turnaround, 2. Profit Improvement, 3. Corporate
Renewal, 4. Organizational Change

Whales Tale Press
P.O. Box 27
Lake Forest, Illinois 60045
1-800-914-1887
www.whalestalepress.com

For Ira Nathanson, good friend. He gave courage.

ACKNOWLEDGEMENTS

To all those CEOs who shared with me the inner lives of their companies and showed me how they worked, I give thanks. You know who you are.

Preface

Quite simply, this book is about corporate results. It is about significantly enlarging profits, about improving performance, about increasing competitiveness. And doing so quickly.

It is about Turnaround. Not late-stage or work-out, but Preemptive and Early Decline Turnaround when the resources of companies are still substantial and credit still available.

It is about changing the innate trajectory of organizations— that part of corporate performance that is independent of the economy or the competition—long before financial crises hit.

And it is about Corporate Renewal, about creating new beginnings.

But this book is also about the fundamental nature of human organizations, as living, breathing entities. It is about the unique, integral personhood of companies. It is about their *Operating Dynamic*, that component of a company that is responsible for its corporate behaviors and performance, that part that is independent of strategy and structure, separate from tactics and finance and process.

And, above all, it is about how, corporate leaders can effect the operating dynamic of their companies and trigger change and recovery, and transformation and growth.

The concepts described here are fundamental. All will intuitively recognize their validity. What makes them unusual, is that, for the first time, they have been articulated and integrated into a practical program any CEO can use to generate corporate transformation and corporate results.

The instruments and processes that comprise the program are themselves profoundly understandable and have been developed and battle tested in companies over the last twenty years and proven on their bottom lines.

Table of Contents

INTRODUCTION

WE WERE DOING SOMETHING RIGHT!

We were in the business of profit improvement, of corporate renewal, of early-decline and preemptive turnaround. We were doing something right! We saw it in the results our clients achieved. We saw it in the enthusiasm, in the fire, of their managers.

We had been in consulting long enough to know that the results we were looking at were unusual for our business, the consistency of the results even more so. And, the renewed fire rarer still.

We knew from experience, and business literature would later bear us out, that most "corporate improvement" programs were disappointing; from MBO to TQM and all the alphabet of programs in between, only a third or thereabouts showed significant—i.e. 10% or better—improvements on the bottom line.

Likewise, we knew that fully two-thirds of mergers and acquisitions were disappointing, if not worse. Again that was something the literature would report—and to this day still does. That success rate of 33% seemed to be some kind of business constant. Even Reengineering, the most recent and acclaimed darling of management programs, shows that same unvarying percentage.

But then it was 1980, we were looking at our clients' results and comparing them. We had opened our practice, under our own shield, four years before, after years with large consulting firms. We had elected to do our work a different way. With a different philosophy. With different expectations.

It was bearing fruit, it seemed. We were enabling clients to achieve better results, more frequently than before. Perhaps twice as often as traditional approaches would provide.

But still, we saw, some clients would not respond. We found eventually it was the companies that did not catch fire, the companies where the management did not grow enthused, were the ones that did not respond, that did not show results. And we did not know why. Not really.

And so, the search for results continued. But now we added to it another search, a search for the factors that would let the spirit of companies catch fire. We guessed that once we knew what these were and could quantify them then we could effect the outcome better. Or tell our clients why they should not even try.

By trial and error, again and again, we changed the way we worked. Always looking at results. Always asking why things worked.

Improvements came. Better results. Quicker results. At less cost in time and effort and dollars. We began referring to bottom line results in terms of multiples of ROI per year, rather than fractions.

But explanations, satisfying explanations, still eluded us.

By 1990 we knew we had created a process that was consistently and reliably enabling clients to radically alter—for themselves—the innate trajectories of their companies. It enabled clients to create surges in performance, especially *systemic* performance, even from initial positions of corporate strength, and to sustain them.

This process also enabled clients to re-ignite within them the entrepreneurial spirit that they had started with. That fire, it seemed, was the core driver of performance.

We were happy about those results, of course; our clients were happy too. After all, in the real world of business results are what is most important. But an explanation would be nice. And we were often asked.

We had, of course, had some epiphanies. But such illuminations come when and where they wish and can not be commanded.

The first major one arrived in 1981. It was at a management conference on Marco Island, in the overheard comments of an irate banker. It explained to us why "strategic" planning didn't work. She was right, we immediately knew, and after that we stopped that kind of work. And moved on.

Our second came the same year at another conference in New York; epiphanies came, it seemed, at conferences that year. There we learned the need all companies have for courage, let's be honest - GUTS, in management; we had thought, it seemed, like many of our consulting kind that analysis was king; or perhaps finance was.

The next came in 1982. We witnessed, close up, the triumphant turnaround of a great US company, a household name, as it pulled back from the brink of insolvency. We saw within it, entire units, high performing units that had never been in trouble, surging in performance and profits and becoming younger, more aggressive, more innovative, along with the units that had been in trouble.

Each year since then, one by one, epiphanies have come—even September 11th brought to us the proud lesson of Giuliani.

One by one we wrote about them. Seeking our own understanding in our written explanations. First in white papers, just for clients. Later, in published articles as the business magazines began to hear about results.

Some of these articles, particularly those that were published multiple times, became the chapters of this book. These address the underlying explanations as we saw them at the time, though only dimly at first.

But, because bottom line results are more important for our clients (and us) than any explanation, each chapter also addresses the PROCESS, how that works, and how to make it work.

We call it The Corporate Renewal Process©.

Its first purpose, and its last, is the improvement of the business AND the bottom line.

How it works is by renewing and revitalizing the overall organization and re-igniting its spirit. And then letting the renewed, reenergized, rekindled organization create the surges in performance for itself.

It is a simple process. Quite simple—as riding a bicycle is simple. And, like riding a bicycle, easier by far to do than to describe in writing. Because so much of the process has components that address the inner drives of the company, to really understand it and really get a sense of it, requires one to both see it as it happens and experience the spirit within the management teams catch fire.

However, to compensate in some small part for this difficulty, the chapters all deal with the process from different perspectives.

But, for the curious among you, why does it work?

Well, over the years our explanations have grown simpler and that suggests we are getting closer to the truth. We believe, that:

- Each company is a living entity, with its own unique personhood, its own operating dynamic, its own spirit. Each has an innate capacity (and instinct) to grow and thrive and heal itself when injured. Just as people have.

- Each corporate entity can be spoken to and touched and changed by those who know how. And in turn can speak and make its needs be known to those who learn to listen.

- The process that we use, The Corporate Renewal Process©, enables CEOs and managing officers and their teams to access this spirit, this essential core of their companies and spark it to catch fire. And cause the fire to trigger change.

- The changed, renewed companies then simply perform differently.

This is what we believe. But belief is not essential for the working of the process; that worked long before we had an explanation. And works for all who use it, belief or not.

But there is just one small caveat, one small requirement:

Within the company, there must be a leader who is ambitious for the company, who has the courage to look deep into that company's soul and have his people look there too; and, who by presence, by word, and by action, gives courage.

Go now and build your fire . . .

Build it in the belly of your company.

And let your company be renewed

Body,

Soul &

Bottom Line.

Simplify the Politics!

I heard him use the term only twice: once, the first time we met, when he hired us to help with the turnaround of his company. He was the newly appointed CEO; his company was large, a household name, with tens of thousands of workers, faltering badly. He used this term to describe the essence of the philosophy he would use to stop the bleeding, to reverse the trends, the downward trajectory. It was the axiom around which he would base his work.

The second time was the last time we met: the project successfully over; the massive hemorrhage of value stopped; the company in the black, again making serious profits; more importantly, alive, vigorous, valuable, competing confidently in its marketplace, to be reckoned with again.

Simplify the Politics!
The First Step of Corporate Renewal

Simplify the politics!

Simplify the politics!

I heard him use the term only twice: once, the first time we met, when he hired us to help with the turnaround of his company. He was the newly appointed CEO; his company was large, a household name, with tens of thousands of workers, faltering badly. He used this term to describe the essence of the philosophy he would use to stop the bleeding, to reverse the trends, the downward trajectory. It was the axiom around which he would base his work.

The second time was the last time we met: the project successfully over; the massive hemorrhage of value stopped; the company in the black, again making serious profits; more importantly, alive, vigorous, valuable, competing confidently in its marketplace, to be reckoned with again.

This second time he described it as the essential core of the management practices he had instilled, that would be used by all managers, from corporate officers to the front line supervisors, in good times and in bad.

He bade us use it in our work.

In between, though, I watched him live it. I heard it often in my head. The phrase had resonated with me powerfully the first time he said it, "Simplify the Politics!" It made so much sense. I had seen its effects in action thousands of times in our practice—more often in the breach, though, than in the observance. With a moral certainty, I knew it to be true. Though I needed him to articulate it for me.

I thought of him using it as a mantra, as he walked his rapid walk between his open office and the offices of his people, their plants, and their warehouses. I heard it whispering in the air as he listened to his workers, or picked up the phone, or wrote a memo. I felt it in his meetings, where the past was being interred, where the future was being claimed.

We did use it in our work. We talked to every CEO we worked with about the concept. All agreed that it was true, that it made sense; once they had thought about it, they knew it to be true.

But we discovered something: few CEOs could actually do it— even with a financial crisis driving its acceptance; in good times, much fewer could do it. Many tried, many made serious and sustained efforts, but somehow they were rebuffed by the culture they inhabited.

The ability to cause this profound simplification seemed to be an innate gift of leadership.

SYSTEMIC IMPROVEMENT

Though rare, it did happen from time to time and when it did, when the politics were simplified, we saw a surge in profits, in business performance—each and every time. A surge that was not dependent on strategic change or altered tactics. A surge that was independent of initial financial condition. A surge that was driven by SYSTEMIC improvement in everything that happened in the company.

The surge occurred very quickly. Systemic change, it seems, has an almost instantaneous effect on performance. It was independent of industry, too.

THE SEARCH

Because the potential benefits to our clients were so great, we kept trying, hoping to find a way that would let a CEO simplify the politics; let any CEO simplify the politics. Eventually, of course, we did. Over the last fifteen years that simplification has become the major focus of our practice.

Some people call what we do Turnaround and it is. But because we commonly use it much earlier in the downward slope, "Preemptive Turnaround" or "Early-Decline Turnaround" are better terms. When we use it in healthy companies where the results are even more remarkable—the majority of our clients—"Profit Improvement" and "Corporate Renewal" are better still.

But the name that is used does not matter. By one name or another the politics are simplified, profits improve and companies are strengthened.

The search was long, often disheartening, and when all came together finally it did so by a series of accidents, coincidences:

First, our office lease was up and we had to move. The files of some two hundred organizations, two hundred managing officers we had worked with, had to be moved or dumped. The latter was the sensible thing to do.

Second, I was in a compulsive, nostalgic mood that year and had to visit all the files again, just one last time—I had not realized just what a pack rat I had been. But visit them I did and for each one wrote down the core issues that had driven events both positive and negative in that organization. There was no theory driving my selection, merely memory. I could see the real issues, it seemed, better in hindsight than at the time.

Some of the issues were financial. Some were the early warning signs of corporate trouble. But the vast majority were the kinds of things that never appeared in the literature of business. A few were downright bizarre.

Third, we had just signed up a new client who wanted to try something different. The company was not in trouble; yet the CEO felt that a significant improvement in performance was achievable and would be needed too. He had a feeling. He had tried all the management programs he could think of and they had not worked.

THE PROGRAM

So we put together a program that was different:

1. The issues culled from our two hundred files were turned into a survey—never mind that most of them had never been considered before as having anything to do with business performance.

2. All the managers and supervisors of the company were given this questionnaire and all responded. (This was in place of the traditional interviews consultants like to conduct; the cost to the client was much less—about a tenth, I think; from our point of view it promised to be less boring.)

3. We held an open feedback session in which the senior managers did the analyses, not us.

In that first feedback day the entire methodology came together. We had found the way to simplify the politics!

We had known for years in our turnaround practice that the financial factors of a company could be ignored, and often were ignored, by management, by the CEO, by the board— until disaster struck. Even after that there would often be denial. That was why we were in business. It is as if financial factors have no power over people's minds. It makes no sense, but that is reality.

We had also known from our due diligence work that the early warning signs are even more ignorable. But again that was why we were in business. What we found now, in that first feedback session, was that the factors we were asking the management team to confront, could not be ignored. The managers did not like the answers they were looking at, but they were fascinated by them. It was as if they were at once both repelled and attracted by them.

They were looking into the dark recesses of the corporate soul, that part of the company they as managers were uniquely responsible for, and were both disgusted and compelled to look. They were looking at that part of the soul that they knew they would have to change if they wanted anything to really change. They would not, could not walk away; though they must have felt a great desire to do so. It was as if the subject matter held its own fascination beyond both the banality of finance and the early warning signs.

Nobody liked what he or she saw. Certainly not the managers. Certainly not the supervisors. The workforce was saying exactly the same—everyone knew that.

Everyone in the room with us was responsible for the behaviors. Everyone had kept on doing them—being them really. Everyone knew that if they could only stop behaving that way, things could be better for them all.

Everyone blamed everyone else—especially those higher up, or over there, or in that other business unit, even the customers. The things they said about each other! Justifiable too, some of them.

THE BUSINESS PERFORMANCE DRIVERS

Later, we were to call these factors the Business Performance Drivers: because they are indeed the cause, the wellspring, and the roots of corporate behavior—the attributes that generate performance. There are more than a hundred of them, each able to impel or retard "depending on its value" organizational performance.

But it also turned out that these drivers have within them the seeds of their own change. They even have within them the motivation for their own transformation.

In the process, the management team viscerally confronting these drivers and in evoking their own emotional responses, in evoking the emotional spirit of the company—they caused the politics to be simplified.

Within a year, in what turned out to a recession for their industry, that company increased its profits by 10%. More importantly, the very operating dynamic of the company was changed.

What were they, what are they, these Performance Drivers? There are more than a hundred, but here I will mention just a few. The most obvious of course is morale, though that is not really important, more a symptom than a driver. Much more important are Corporate (in)Decisiveness, Acknowledgment of Work, Communication of Vision, Integrity of Management, Relationships of Managers. (A fuller list is available through our website http://www.ManagementConsultants.com)

THE PROCESS OF SIMPLIFICATION

That first day it was our client who created the process, not us. It is as if the process was there, implicit in the questions and the responses, waiting to be uncovered. Since then we have improved and modified it. Technology has made everything happen faster, better, cheaper, as it should. But the process that came together then, is still recognizably the same.

What was the process? Simply stated, the CEO and the management team looked at their own responses and the responses of their people, and on each and every issue, asked themselves these questions:

— What is the real answer?
— How do we *FEEL* about this?
— What should we be?
— What do we commit to do to achieve it?
— What will I (by name) do? When? Who will check it?

At first there was a sense of helplessness and hopelessness that pervaded everything and everybody. Nobody knew how to break through. Individually they had all known what the matter was, and what the results could be. Everyone had said so to everyone else, one-on-one. But it was as if the collective, the entity personified by the management team, had not heard, and so was condemned to going on as if it were deaf, unknowing—in a corporate trance.

But the corporate entity, the spirit of the company, was now confronting the issues. We were merely the process catalysts. We watched the transformations happen. Because that was what was happening: Transformation!

The mechanics of the process are easy to describe. They consist of the survey instrument and responses and the questions asked of the managers that appear above.

What happens within the process is very difficult to explain to those who have not undertaken it, because feelings are what drive it—not the action steps themselves.

We did not have words for it then, but later we were told that the classic process of human spiritual-emotional transformation had been applied to a corporate entity:

> First there was revulsion, collective revulsion, at what they were seeing—denial was not possible, nor wanted.

> Then there was an emotional discharge: *Catharsis.*

> Then an immediate investment/commitment of that same energy into a new vision of the company, a new way of being: *Cathexis.*

The room was filled with energy that had to be channeled, that was being channeled. We were out of the business of cerebral consulting into renewal of the corporate spirit.

Then something else began to happen. Quite spontaneously, the team began to take on the early warning signs that no one had wanted to address before.

Everyone in the business world knows that the entire management team of a company must be as one on each of the warning signs. Early Warning Signs are leading and collateral expressions of performance. If the team members are not together, they will be making conflicting decisions, or worse, bad decisions. Think of the disparate decisions that can be made from conflicting views of the cash flow position. Cash flow is just one. There are fifty other warning signs.

It turned out the managers were all over the board on these. They had not understood the financials all that well either, but no one had wanted to admit it until then.

Actions were accepted, in writing, by each and every manager, by name, so that each and every issue of consequence would be taken into final resolution.

The energy invested into the new beginning, the cathexis, had come initially from the revulsion with the old. It was coming out of the politics that were getting simpler.

Soon energy was creating itself from sheer delight with the vision of the new that was being generated. That was being invested too, creating still more ideas. Action steps were accepted, written down, and committed to, implement these new ideas too. Then it was over. The company was different. It was different in a most profound way: the misunderstandings, the animosities, the lies, the reluctancies were gone, burned out in the fire of the process.

The politics were simplified; in over a hundred different ways they were simplified.

The management team was together; the company was as one.

It is not really hard to do, this simplifying of politics—once you know it can be done, certainly not after you have seen it done.

It makes money for the company like nothing else that we have seen, and quickly. Costs, even when using facilitators, are minimal; a first year ROI of 20:1 or better should be expected.

It leaves the company stronger, always stronger, healthier, more assertive. A better place in which to work and lead.

All it takes is a CEO with the desire to make things sharply better, a CEO with the courage to make the managers look deep into the soul of their company and not flinch away, a CEO who will say, quietly, day after day:

Simplify the politics!

Simplify the politics!

And do so.

Mirror, Mirror, on the Wall...

Within a company, no great change can happen, no sustainable performance increase can be achieved unless and until that company faces what it really is, clearly and fearlessly.

Each month, each quarter, each year, professionally managed companies review their financial performance and their management reports. Occasionally, they will augment this with a "due diligence audit" of the early warning signs—as if it were to be sold or bought.

Yet all the factors looked at in these examinations account for no more than 10% of bottom line performance. Because everything looked at is history, expressions of performance. Even early warning signs are expressions of performance, not causes.

The factors causing the other 90% of corporate performance are not addressed.

These are the Drivers of Corporate Performance. Most lie hidden within the emotional life of the company. Collectively they form its Operating Dynamic.

The challenge each CEO faces is coming to grips with this Operating Dynamic: identifying its elements—the Performance Drivers; evaluating their effects on the company; and purposefully transforming them.

There are more than one hundred Drivers. All of them impel performance. But there are five major ones. As these change, so directly and immediately does the performance of the company.

Mirror, Mirror, on the Wall...
On Facing Corporate Reality

It was not pornography, well not exactly, though it did fascinate. It dealt with primal urge, and potency and creation and genesis. It did inspire guilt and caused each of them a kind of embarrassment—that others should see them looking, like voyeurs. Even Harry, who had spent hours with it, found it so.

No it was not pornography. But they sat there, fascinated, silent and ashamed, just staring... Harry did not speak. He waited.

George said again: "But it can't be that bad. We're doing all right." He had said it at least ten times that morning. But now it was empty of denial. Just a reflex. The silence stretched.

Eventually (it seemed forever in the silence, but it was just moments) George spoke again: "This must be who we are. God help us!" A sentiment that Harry shared. He had said much the same the night before as he studied the picture.

There it was, staring them in the face, writ large upon the wall. Not deniable now; for they had tried repeatedly that morning to deny it and they had failed.

They were an accident waiting to happen.

Harry was the CEO. George, the CFO. They, with the other seven were the entire management team.

They were looking at their company, as they had never seen it before. Never so completely nor so clearly. In the cold, implacable mirror of their own answers, of their own words.

Naked it lay, without disguise. Everything on view, not just the usual financials or even the early warning signs or the unobtrusive measures, but also its demons, its drives, its motivations, the very wellsprings of its performance. The secrets they had known, but had never spoken of. And secrets too they had not known.

They were an accident waiting to happen.

George said again, a little plaintively and still puzzled: "But we're making money, aren't we!?"

This time Harry responded: "Yes! But for how long? One bad blow and we're in trouble. We're fragile in ways I hadn't imagined. And the economy is beginning to slow."

He lapsed into silence again, letting it work. And waited...

Then Alice spoke, their EVP of sales and, in her own quite way, their bravest warrior. She simply said: "What are we going to do about it?"

Until just a few years ago, this in-depth illumination of the heart and soul of a company would never have been possible; the instruments did not exist, and neither did the techniques for transmuting the understanding gained into commitment or the knowledge gained into action. (Such clear vision, such intense drive to action, usually happens only in extreme financial crisis.) But Harry and his team did look deeply in and saw what was really there. They did so without fear. They caused change, great change, and did so without danger.

Within a company, no great change can happen, no substantial performance increase can be achieved unless and until that company faces fearlessly (fearfully will do at a pinch) and clearly what it is today, especially its inner life—that life that drives performance and results.

Each month, each quarter, each year, professionally managed companies review their financial performance and their management reports. Occasionally, they will augment this with a "due diligence audit" of the early warning signs—as if it were to be sold or bought.

Yet all the factors looked at in these examinations account for no more than 10% of bottom line performance, because everything looked at is historic, *mere expressions* of performance. Even the earliest of early warning signs are expressions of performance, not causes.

The factors causing the other 90% of corporate performance are not addressed.

There are three broad categories of factors that describe a company:

The Usual. Those that commonly appear on the financials and management reports; these we all know.

The Early Warning Signs. These are the leading performance indicators, the unobtrusive measures of performance, collateral expressions of performance. These are the meat and potatoes of due diligence audits. Examples might be Cash Flow or Market Share. There are more than fifty of these. They can be measured objectively either by people within the company or by outsiders. Refer to the Appendix for a list.

The Drivers of Performance. These are the factors that are the real cause and motivation of the behavior of managers and the performance of the company. Most lie hidden within the emotional life of the company. Collectively they form its *Operating Dynamic.* The challenge each CEO faces is coming to grips with this Operating Dynamic: identifying its elements—the Performance Drivers; evaluating their effects on the company; and purposefully transforming them. Refer to the Appendix for a list.

There are, in all, more than a hundred of these Performance Drivers: from Assertiveness, to Acknowledgement of Work, to Corporate Decisiveness, to Morale, to Zeal. All of them, to greater or lesser extent, are causes, motive factors, forcing functions. They effect individual behavior directly and immediately, corporate performance indirectly and quickly, and bottom line soon after that.

For, when a driver is changed, individual behavior is changed. When behavior is changed, performance is changed. When performance is changed, so is the bottom-line changed.

Everyone on Harry's team was familiar with the financials so they touched on them only briefly. There were no surprises there.

With the Leading Performance Indicators, though, they were less familiar. When Harry and George had bought the company some fifteen years before they had done a rigorous due diligence, but they had not thought to do one since; such in-depth reviews are expensive and time consuming. However, the thought of getting the opinion of their managers on what a due diligence might reveal, was intriguing.

THE CORPORATE 360° SURVEY

To prepare for their retreat—the Due Diligence Management Retreat—all levels of management within the company were asked to respond (anonymously) to a web-based questionnaire, The Corporate 360° Survey . This would provide a 360° appraisal of the company as a whole, from within, through the eyes and with the perspective of its managers, those who were most responsible for its current condition, those who would have to bear the burden of changing the company if it needed changing.

The survey and the responses of the managers would provide the mirror in which the company would see its face. Harry would hold the mirror. The managers would look.

This survey contained questions on about forty of the due diligence elements. They included: Cash Flow, Sales, Market Share, Quality, and Inventory Trends. A fuller list of elements is included in the Appendix.

Then the senior team talked about them. They knew that unless they all agreed on what the value of these elements were, the decisions they were making were probably in conflict. They assumed they would be mainly in concert on these.

It was scary, or it should have been. Only on four of the fifty issues were the managers as one: not on cash flow; not on market share; not on quality; not in their relationship with their bankers; not on the relationship with their customers.

For many of the issues there were definite answers available and the first part of the session was spent just in bringing all the team into alignment. They saw immediately that just resolving two or three key differences of opinion could bring hundreds of thousands of dollars to the bottom line. It gave them a sense that they were doing something immediately valuable.

But somehow discussions on these did not lead to any great emotional commitment to do anything about them—by anyone except Harry. At least he liked to think they motivated him. Somehow, it is the nature of these indicators to neither touch the soul or the emotions of people, nor to impel action. This makes no sense. It is not logical, but it is why so many early decline turnarounds come to nothing.

Then they addressed the Drivers. A hundred of these were included in the Corporate 360°. Quite purposefully, these had been shown lower down on the survey.

In world class companies, very few of these drivers (usually less than a dozen) show problems. And then at just moderate to low levels. Overtly troubled companies, that have been experiencing distress for some time, show many more—as many as sixty or seventy and at high levels of intensity. *So also do companies that are about to have problems.*

These Drivers not only cause performance; they are the true predictors of performance.

The managers had responded to questions on a hundred of these drivers and Harry and his team had identified problems in more than forty. Twenty of those were three star (***) issues (out of five) or greater. And five turned out to be five star (*****) issues: issues that were sucking the energy and drive and creativity out of the company and out of its managers; issues that had been growing, unseen, in the soul of the company; issues that had to be dealt with, not just intellectually, but also emotionally. And not just by the managers individually, but also by the team as a whole, by the very company itself.

Three of the five star issues were in the top ten of (un)popular corporate cancers, two were unusual. But to this company it was absolutely critical that they be resolved if the company were to move on. They were:

- Corporate Decisiveness
- Corporate Aging
- Acknowledgement of Work
- Conflict Resolution
- Assertiveness

Other (for this company, lesser) issues included:

- Loyalty
- Office Politics
- Planning
- Communication
- Customer Orientation
- Sharing of Corporate Vision

The process and style of addressing and resolving corporate issues, both five star and lesser, is dealt with in other chapters. Suffice it to say here, Harry and his team did it well. They looked in the mirror; they stared into the soul of their company and did not flinch.

The key issues were all resolved and taken into commitment and action within just two days. Within two weeks the other management ranks were involved and two weeks later the changed behavior of management had begun to show in performance.

Changing the Drivers had changed the Indicators. For example, in Harry's case, changing the Communications driver changed the Cash Flow indicator, amongst others. Another example, changing the Sharing-of-Corporate-Vision driver reduced the Absenteeism indicator. And naturally, changing the indicators changed the bottom line.

One year later, having dodged a bullet that could have and would have hurt them badly, they showed a 10% increase in profits. The return on the investment they had made in their "mirror" was 30:1.

The "mirror" is without mystery: the diagnostic instrument and its questions, once seen, are immediately understood; the process of looking, of addressing the issues, once it is experienced, is so profoundly simple it can be led by any manager.

And there is no magic; except in the results.

Mirror! Mirror! On the Wall!

Who is the fairest one of all?

The Company: Living Entity or Machine?

People have always known instinctively that a human enterprise is a living, breathing entity that grows and ages, sickens
and heals, flourishes and fails. It is something that is organic
in nature. It has personality and the ability to learn and to
reproduce. It has personhood. It is something that is much
greater than the sum of its functions. It is much different than
the sum of its people.

Entrepreneurial and charismatic leaders have always known
this quite intuitively and use it to lead, motivate and transform
their companies. They use their organizations' living energies
to magnify their leadership and their ambition for their companies. They alter elements of their companies' inner lives to
force changes in the externals. They may not talk about it for
many would be too embarrassed, but they think about their
companies as persons.

Repeatedly over the last twenty years we have watched managing officers intuitively use these steps to turnaround
companies and transform their performance. Frequently we
have used these steps ourselves to enable companies to sharply
increase their profits and renew themselves.

The Company: Living Entity or Machine?
How You Treat It Determines Its Performance

People have always known instinctively that a human enterprise is a living, breathing entity that grows and ages, sickens and heals, flourishes and fails. It is something that is organic in nature. It has personality and the ability to learn and to reproduce. It has personhood. It is something that is much greater than the sum of its functions. It is much different than the sum of its people.

This personhood is most easily recognized at both ends of the spectrum of corporate success. World-class companies exhibit a character of focus, power, and oneness that is palpable even to a casual visitor. Companies in deep distress show a personality that is equally vivid but fragmented, fearful, and impotent.

All companies have this personhood, whether it is strong or weak, potent or ineffective, motivating or destructive. These corporate personae have inner lives at least as complex and as richly tapestried as people do. Not only do these inner lives coexist with the external results of corporate success and failure, but also actually precede and cause them. In our work, we find about 150 attributes of corporate personality that can cause, effect or predict bottom-line performance.

Entrepreneurial and charismatic leaders have always known this quite intuitively and use it to lead, motivate and transform their companies. They use their organizations' living energies to magnify their leadership and their ambition for their companies. They alter elements of their companies' inner lives to force changes in the externals. They may not talk about it for many would be too embarrassed, but they think about their companies as persons.

For more than eighty years, definitely since the advent of "scientific management", the company-as-machine paradigm has become the model most used. It is used particularly when growing, changing or improving organizations is attempted.

Unquestionably, such a model has its uses. Certainly it is easy to teach and understand. Undoubtedly it lends itself to ready analysis. It also has profound limitations. It is as limited as the model of a human body without its life, without its spirit.

Changing the inert, spiritless human body can only be done mechanically. The results can be no more than was done to it. The body without its life can offer no response, no help. It has no ability to further what has been done to it. Decay is the only possible result.

Trying to change a company in any significant way using the company-as-machine model is like that. Business Process Reengineering is a prime example. It is successful only about 30% of the time, a percentage comparable to that of a placebo effect. Trying to change it by coaching one person at a time is even less successful.

However, so pervasive has the company-as-machine model become that many managers and consultants act as if it is the only one available. When asked, they may speak about the company as a living entity. But even then they are thinking of it as its culture or the sum of its people.

This machine approach to corporate change is most often seen in the more established and more bureaucratic companies. In entrepreneurial organizations it appears more rarely. When the machine approach does appear, the company ceases to be entrepreneurial.

But an alternative to this company-as-machine model exists. The company can be dealt with as a person possessing life, body, and soul. Treating the company this way allows it (actually, forces it) to respond as a thinking, competing organism to its leadership, its people, and its marketplace. Treating the company as a person evokes its personhood and simultaneously evokes attributes only living creatures have. These attributes include the ability to adapt and heal, to grow and flourish, to change and even transform.

It takes a leader, as opposed to an administrator, to evoke this living response. While it would be nice for all companies to have leaders who have the instinct and charisma to do this, it is not needed. A body of knowledge and practice exists that allows any CEO to address the organization as an entity and mobilize it, cause it to change, cause it to heal. The process works quickly and almost without effort because this approach draws upon the company's innate instinct to heal and to succeed.

As with all fundamental techniques of leadership the process is profoundly simple like walking or riding a bicycle. Like walking and cycling it is almost impossible to analyze. It is difficult to explain in words. But the knowledge that it can be done coupled with a little help and practice makes it so easy to learn.

As a CEO there are just three major steps, constantly repeated, that you need to take. Perfection is not needed and the steps become more effective with practice.

The first step makes the others easy and natural. Visualize the company as a person. See it. Hear it. Feel it as an entity. Personify it. Give it form, shape, and color within your mind. Identify its personality both as it is and as it should be. The more vividly you do this the more effective the other steps will be.

The second step is to evoke the company. The most successful technique to do this is to call the management team together. Whenever the management team is knowingly and purposefully making decisions for the business, the company is there too. As you talk with the management team, remain aware that you talk with the company too. As you decide with them for the company's sake, you decide with it too. Saying to the group (and the company), "We are the company", is a powerful, empowering evocation. Also, whenever you talk to your workers about the company, which should be often, speak to the company through them and listen to the company through them.

The third step is to increase the company's power, its potency, and its authority. Embolden it. Embolden it enough for it to make known its needs and its potential above and in spite of the prejudices and preferences of individuals on the management team and even the CEO's prejudices and preferences.

Simplifying the politics of the company is the way to do this. The simpler the politics and the clearer the focus, the more powerful becomes the spirit of the company. As the company grows in potency and in clarity, workers at all levels begin to respond to it as a separate entity. Creativity grows. Morale improves. The organization becomes more responsive to leadership. Leadership draws on the inspiration, knowledge, and energy of its workers. The key factors of the inner life of the company come into balance. External changes follow.

Repeatedly, over the last twenty years we have watched managing officers intuitively use these steps to turnaround companies and transform their performance. Frequently, we have used these steps ourselves to enable companies to sharply increase their profits and renew themselves.

The steps may seem a little mystical, but they are as real as riding a bicycle. It will take you just a little time and effort to begin them properly. With practice they will become innate and the results will occur faster. Once started, it takes no time from your day and the results of the normal course of business are magnified.

Treating the company as a living entity, causes it to be so, to become more so. The more definite its personhood becomes, the more it flourishes.

It happens first within the heart and mind of the CEO. No one else need ever know.

Fire in the Corporate Belly

It is the spirit of the company which must catch fire—it can be touched, changed, and **ignited**.

There are many reasons why a company ages. But for whatever reason, this aging manifests itself in bureaucracy, boredom, introversion, timidity, stiff formality, and above all, lack of fire. Unless this fire is re-ignited the company falters, slows, and finally dies.

But companies, unlike people, can be immortal—or nearly so. Companies, with the right leadership, with the right stimulus, can slow and stop and reverse the aging process. And it must happen again and again, if it is to compete, if it is to create, if it is to endure.

This reignition of corporate fire, this rekindling of fighting spirit, this rejuvenation of the enterprise, must be the work of the CEO.

It has long been thought that such renewal can only happen with new management, but that is no longer the case. Simple techniques for reigniting the competitive spirit now exist and they have been proven time and again on the bottom-lines of companies both large and small.

They can be used by any CEO with ambition and the will to have his managers look deep into the soul, into the operating dynamic, of their company. And not flinch away.

Fire in the Corporate Belly
Reversing the Corporate Aging Process

THE COMPANY JUST FELT OLD. It was under twenty, but it felt old. That was our first impression. It felt cold too. Nothing you could put your finger on, but there was no excitement in the faces of the people we saw.

Ron was the CEO. We talked with him about his challenges. They were frustrations mostly. He spoke of the past. He had founded his company nineteen years before. For the first few years there was innovation, growth, exhilaration, and sheer excitement for everyone who worked there. Its strong roots penetrated the industry it served.

But the last few years were different: growth had slowed; there had been few new products and they were really me-too copies of the competition's products; profits were still OK. But the company was no longer the darling of the analysts. The people who had grown with the company were still there, but their fire had gone out. There was no trouble that he could see, but something was not right. He wanted a vibrant company again.

He had tried everything he knew: management and leadership courses; team building sessions; counseling with psychologists; expensive reengineering that never showed on the bottom line; and strategic planning, too. He talked of stepping down. Would a new CEO make a difference? One of his outside board members had very tactfully raised the subject. But the message was clear. The company had plateaued, maybe had lost its way. Certainly it had lost its drive.

We asked how badly he wanted the company to flourish again. We listened to his manner and his tone more than his words. For not all managing officers who believe they want resurgence, really do. There can be a narcotic comfort in the familiar, especially if there is no immediate financial pain. Renewal brings uncertainty, but he wanted renewal. We could hear it. He would be able to look into the soul of his company and not blink.

A week later his managers and supervisors got a questionnaire. It asked their opinions on all sorts of issues—some unexpected, some puzzling, some disturbing.

Two weeks after that he called his management team together, off site. Together they faced their answers and the answers of their subordinates. A bright mirror was being held so that they could not look away. In it they saw their company, they saw their divisions, they saw themselves, as they really were. In one way or another, they said: "This is who we are! God help us!" Then their work began.

QUENCHING THE SPIRIT

There are many reasons why the fighting spirit of a company can be quenched besides the obvious ones like a protected marketplace, continued reversals, and a maturing industry. One way or another, they result in an aging company. That more than anything else, dims, extinguishes its competitive fire, and it slows.

But companies, unlike people, can be immortal—or nearly so. Companies can stop and reverse the aging process. Chronological age of companies can differ from competitive age. The youth or senescence, vigor or lethargy, of these companies has little connection with years.

This aging manifests itself in a number of ways. Bureaucracy, boredom, introversion, timidity, sloth and stiff formality, are some. But corporate sclerosis is the result, and lack of fire.

The Challenge for Management becomes the periodic reversal of aging, the rekindling of the fighting spirit of the company;

the turning around, preferably before it is necessary, of the business.

But, to change anything as fundamental as psychological age, as the way a company sees and responds to the world, something fundamental within it must change. Its very spirit must change. Must catch fire. Must renew.

As surely as a person has a spirit, something that is more than personality, so does a company. It is this spirit which must catch fire.

What the spirit of a company is does not really matter. What matters is that it can be touched, changed, and ignited—very directly and very easily.

The Spirit of the Company, its fighting spirit, resides mostly within the senior management of the company, especially in the *Relationships* between the senior managers. It exists when these managers, as a group, as a team, act as the organization's essential core. It exists whether they know it or not, whether the team is aware of itself as the core or not, and whether anyone admits there is a spirit or not. This spirit expresses itself in the emotional drive, worldview, philosophy, attitude, and performance of the managers and the company.

One way to change this spirit is to change the management team, starting with the CEO, and hoping the new team will have the drive and fire that is needed. This is what is usually attempted in a crisis driven turnaround, but short of a major catastrophe, changing the people is seldom necessary.

There is another other way to change the spirit of the company: change the *Relationships* within the team and the team's relationship with the company. Done properly, the company is renewed, the fighting spirit is reignited, and the company catches fire.

Fortunately, changing relationships is easy under the right circumstances, but only if the managing officer leads; it cannot be done by a subordinate. A crisis is not needed. Charisma is not needed either. The only prerequisite is a CEO who is ambitious for his company and will lead his people in facing the truth.

For rekindling to take place, just seven things need to happen:

1.   The members of the management team (or what is supposed to be the management team) must become in fact the spirit, the soul, and the essential center of the company. The Team must become self aware, conscious of itself as that, and must believe in and acknowledge its authority as that soul.

2.   The management team, now a true Team, must see and acknowledge the company and themselves exactly as it is, exactly as they are; *especially the corporate and human (emotional) drivers of performance.* They must do this both as the soul of the company and as individuals.

3.   The Team must generate a real, visceral revulsion against those factors within the company that it does not like. Individuals must share in this. A catharsis happens. Energy for change, for a new beginning is released.

4.   The Team must define for the company, for itself, a new and detailed business blueprint. A blueprint that defines not just the usual strategies, tactics, goals, and objectives, but also the *spirit* of the company. The team here defines *itself* in terms, as much different and greater than "culture" as the human soul is different and greater than psychology.

5.   From the energy of catharsis, always great, always intense, the Team must create within itself a powerful *emotional* investment in this new future, in this new blueprint. Detail by detail. Corporate and emotional driver by corporate and emotional driver.

6.   Again, with that same energy, the Team must commit, viscerally and emotionally, both as the soul of the company and as individuals, to explicit actions to achieve each and every element of the business blueprint, and commit to full accountability.

7. Implementation and follow-up must begin *immediately.* No time lost.

Ron began the process for his company by arranging for a detailed, in-depth, diagnostic of the company, its divisions and its departments. He hired us to be his Business Catalysts and we prepared a questionnaire.

The questionnaire was specifically designed to be answered by managers, supervisors and senior key staff, not workers. It addressed some 150 factors that underlie, cause, and predict the performance of companies. Some obvious and traditional, some dealing with the soul, the essence of the company. All recipients were told of the importance of the instrument and strongly "encouraged" to respond. This would be a 360° appraisal of the company, from within, through the eyes of those who were responsible, through the eyes of those who would be responsible for the future.

The CEO and we together made the first diagnostic cut. It was immediately obvious that the company was in trouble.

A high performing, world class company, sure of its power and its potency will find some thirty items it does not like about itself, and perhaps one or two "gut" issues that must be dealt with in and through the emotional life of the company if they are to transform, to release the energy of renewal. In Ron's company some seventy items were found. Four or five were gut issues. Twenty or so were "three star". There was no doubt: the company was an accident waiting to happen.

What had to change was clear. What had to be done was clear. But, for the transformation of the company to actually happen, without firing half or more of the senior management, the Team had to come into existence and that Team would have to do all the rest. **There was no team.** That showed in twelve different ways and everyone in management knew. Even Ron! Yes, the company was aging fast: The Psychological Age Index was high.

There was no report generated. That was part of the agreement. (Reports get shelved, especially uncomfortable reports. And this process would not give them the option of shelving anything.) Ron would not leak the results either. They, his managers, would do the analysis, would face the reality of the company, cold, and in the process come together with him to form the soul of the company.

They met off site in a darkened room that had no tables. Just an arc of straight-backed chairs facing two overhead projector screens. There they would see their own answers and the answers of their subordinates. In that room they would wrestle with the meaning of those answers; with the impact of what they saw on the performance of the company, on the performance of themselves. They would be in the deep end with nowhere to go but through. Being brave is easier when there is no option.

After the necessary learning on the lesser issues, the intensity mounted. The "three star" issues were dealt with frontally. Later, the "gut" issues. Slowly, piece by piece, a business blueprint developed. We held the mirror so they could not hide. After a little while they would not attempt to hide

Time after time, Ron asked: "What's the real answer?" The average or the mean did not matter. Real was what they agreed it was. They held the mirror for each other; helped each other see. And, just in case they did not, we were there to wear the black hat and brook no easy denial. They answered. And it was the cold truth. The whole truth. Time after time, we triggered catharsis, releasing energy into the room.

Time after time, Ron asked: "OK, What must it be in two years? **I ask you, ...!**" For emphasis he had borrowed TV newsman John McLaughlin's mannerisms just for the occasion.

Again they answered. Their words appeared before their eyes on the screen, dominating their field of view. Slowly, piece by piece, a business blueprint developed. Piece by piece, they committed—Emotionally! Viscerally! Ritually! Our work now was focused on causing them to invest the energies that had just been released into a commitment to a new way of being, into a new future. Momentum now played a major part of the process.

Soon a clear, appealing picture of the future developed that attracted and excited their interest, their involvement, their commitment. Soon they passed beyond their embarrassments, their revulsions, and were actively hunting for, lobbying for, their picture of the future. Committing. Demanding commitment of each other. Ron too. He loved it.

Time after time, he asked:

"What's the action?" They told him!

"Who'll do it?" They told him!

"When'll it be done?" They told him!

"OK! Can I review on....?" They agreed!

Everything they said appeared before their eyes on the screen, and dominated their field of view. All was transferred to their computer network as an on-line action plan for everyone to see.

They pledged achievement. Before their boss. Before their peers. Before subordinates. Before the very soul of their company.

They delivered! It would have been be impossible not to. They had not left themselves the option of failure. Emotionally, they had burned their bridges.

One year later, four old products were being phased out, five new products were being developed, and one new product was actively being sold. Growth was up.

Once again, there was Fire in the Corporate Belly.

THE POST ACQUISITION DUE DILIGENCE

More than two-thirds of all mergers and acquisitions fail to produce anticipated results. Yet in every case a most careful and thorough due diligence had been done before the investment was made.

However, the very best due diligence possible can, by custom and tradition, look only at certain factors. These factors account for only a fraction of the long-term success of a company—which of course accounts for so many disappointments. To make things worse, the acts of putting companies up for sale and performing due diligence work on them inevitably causes trauma.

Seriously improving the odds of success requires getting a deep and detailed understanding of the actual drivers of corporate behavior—the root causes of long term performance.

Until just a few years ago, such an in-depth illumination of the heart and soul of a company would not have been possible; the instruments did not exist. Nor did the techniques for transmuting the understanding gained into commitment or the knowledge gained into action, but now they do.

With the investor present, the management team can look deeply into the operating dynamic of their company and see what is really there—and do so in time to cause change.

For the investor, it is a *Post-Acquisition Due Diligence©*; for the management team, it is a New Beginning.

The Post Acquisition Due Diligence
The End of the Acquisition

His stomach sent him the signal first. A rumble, a mere rumble.

Harry's was a large stomach, a faithful stomach. One he had lived with a long and trusted time, one he listened to when it spoke. Now it had. A rumble, a mere rumble. But he had heard.

Harry was Group President. One of five such GPs. His job was the purchase, care, and nurturing of acquisitions on behalf of his holding company, a conglomerate. He had held this job a long and trusted time, longer than he had his stomach, almost. He was good. He knew he was good.

He had just bought a company. He had put the word out, found a target company, performed an in-depth due diligence on it, negotiated the price, and finally bought it.

Now, three months later, looking at the early returns in the financials, his stomach was sending an alert. It was just a rumble, a mere rumble; it was, after all, early days yet and there were many reasons for the numbers he was seeing. But he was listening.

The opportunity to buy had came originally, as most such opportunities came to him these days, by referral; he was well known; his company was well known. The opportunity did interest him.

So he looked. Looked deep and long with a due diligence that was thorough and careful. Looked into every aspect of the company that custom and tradition allowed—into the financials, into the operations. He used all the lists, tricks, and techniques prescribed by that most comprehensive authority on due diligence available, the Sahakian Checklists©.

But now he knew, with a moral certainty, that it was time to look much deeper, look into its soul. Look now, before whatever it was his stomach warned about grew worse. He would never have a better time to shape the future than right now. Anyway he had made it clear that it was his practice to look deeper once the acquisition was final—so no one need feel targeted or especially distrusted.

First he called his boss, the holding company CEO; he was confident in himself and in his judgment and felt no embarrassment. "We'll be doing our Post-Acquisition Due Diligence© on the new company this week" was all he really said. There was no need for more; "Best do it now," was a favorite expression of his boss.

He called his new subordinate, George, the CEO of the acquisition, and said, "It's time." Oh, he said it nicely, he said it with all that warm, helpful authority an acquiring executive can muster early in the relationship. With George he did not call it the Post-Acquisition Due Diligence©. No, he called it by its public name The New Beginnings Survey©.

Of course the thought was well received; he hardly had to twist an arm at all. Or mention that the survey would take the executives merely a half an hour or so, and they could break that up to five minutes twice a day if they liked. Anyway George would feel so much better knowing how his people felt after the natural trauma of the acquisition, wouldn't he? "Get it out and get it over with," Harry always said.

He could have it done next week? Well, OK, the week after. So the date was set.

So it began.

That very day, George received draft e-mails he could tailor and send to his managers and supervisors, announcing The New Beginnings Survey©. It was to help them put the past behind and hit the ground running in their new environment.

There were three such e-mails: one to foretell the coming of the survey, explain its importance and its anonymity, and to exhort them to reserve the time; the second, to ask the managers and supervisors to complete it within a week; and another to remind them to get it done and give them the inevitable day or so more that always seems to be required. The first e-mail went out that day to all the managers and supervisors

The following day he had unit and department passwords and the email addresses they would be sent to. This had taken a mere thirty minutes, between the survey firm and his HR officer. Then he issued the second email. To be exact, his secretary did all the hard work in this, over his signature.

One week later, George was able to learn how many had responded, and in what units and departments. Then he issued the follow up reminder, his secretary made a few judicious calls to the tardier areas, and it was done.

THE SURVEY

The survey had been substantial, but it took only thirty or forty minutes to respond in all—except for the inevitable few who invariably had to agonize.

There were really no excuses his people could use for not doing it. The survey was web based and could be accessed from anywhere. It could be answered a few questions or a few minutes at a time. All the questions were couched as statements so there was little need to agonize; the mind presented the answers almost automatically and the responses were made by clicking on a button.

It was also anonymous too—within units. When managers and supervisors accessed the web site they were asked for their unit password and then given a personal and private access number they could use to return to the questionnaire if they wished to interrupt their responses.

At the end, commentary could be added if desired. Many people did.

The survey covered some of the elements the pre-acquisition due diligence had covered; comparing the outside findings with the opinions of the management is always illuminating, for everyone concerned.

It also addressed about one hundred Drivers of Performance. These are the human and organizational factors that underlie, impel and drive the corporate behaviors that generate performance. They are the factors that set the innate trajectory of the company. The innate trajectory is that combination of corporate direction and momentum, independent of the economy and the competition, that predicts the long term future of the company—unless it is purposefully changed.

Two weeks from the day Harry had made his decision, the survey was concluded. All the senior team and 85% of all the others had responded. The survey responses were downloaded by the consultants and reviewed. Two days later, they were ready for a private and off-the-record heads-up with Harry.

He knew the drill; he had a LCD projector ready. In the quietness of the conference room he sat to see what kind of company and issues he had bought.

He knew he had due-diligenced well. But tradition and custom had not permitted him to ask them to take this survey; not a survey that asked questions like this. Now the results were in.

Each time he did this it was different, each company was different. Yet each time it was the same too. The act of being put up for sale, being due-diligenced, (to management that had become a four-letter word) and being bought would traumatize the company being sold. The longer the process, the greater and deeper would be the trauma. This one had gone on, it seemed; he was now looking at the responses—the hurts, the feelings, and the fears.

He was also looking at deeper issues too, not triggered by the sale and acquisition. Things that had been in the psyche of the company for years. Things that even George had probably not been really conscious of, or had no names for, or thought could not be changed and so pushed from his mind and so endured.

But now, in conjunction with the traumas of the sale and the due diligence itself, those negative drivers were conspiring to tilt the trajectory of the company sharply downwards. From experience, long and bitter, Harry knew they would not change themselves. The issues would not go away by ignoring them or giving them more time. They would have to be exposed and diagnosed, taken out, looked at, and deplored. Actions would need to be specifically taken to change them to something better.

It would have to be done, Harry knew, by the company itself. He could not do it for them. Above all, it would have to be done now.

MIRROR, MIRROR, ON THE WALL!

It was not pornography. Well not exactly, though it did fascinate. It dealt with primal urge, potency, and creation. It did inspire guilt and caused each of them a kind of embarrassment that others should see them looking, like voyeurs.

No it was not dirty picture. Just a sad one. But they sat there, fascinated, silent and embarrassed, just staring... Harry did not speak. He waited.

George said again: "But it can't be that bad. We're doing all right." He had said it at least ten times that morning, but now it was empty of denial. Just a reflex. The silence stretched.

Eventually (it seemed forever in the silence, but it was just moments) George spoke again: "This must be who we are. God help us!" A sentiment that Harry shared. He had said much the same, but more colorfully, the week before as he studied the picture.

There it was, staring them in the face, writ large upon the wall. Not deniable now; for they had tried repeatedly that morning to deny it to themselves and they had failed.

They were an accident waiting to happen. Harry privately thought it was an accident already happening.

They were looking at their company as they had never seen it before. Never so completely nor so clearly. In the cold, implacable mirror of their own answers, of their own words. Naked it lay, without disguise. Everything on shameless view, not just the factors the due diligence had disclosed, but also its demons, its drives, its motivations—the very wellsprings of its performance—the secrets they had known, and secrets too they had not known.

They were an accident waiting to happen. They really were. They had said so.

George said again, a little plaintively and still puzzled: "But we're making money, aren't we!?"

This time Harry responded: "Yes! But for how long? It hasn't shown much yet, but the trend is down. One bad blow and we're in trouble. We're fragile in ways I hadn't imagined."

He lapsed into silence again, letting it work. And waited...

Then Alice spoke, their EVP of sales and, in her own quite way, their bravest warrior. She simply said, "What are we going to do about it?"

So they decided, they took action.

Until just a few years ago, this in-depth illumination of the heart and soul of a company would never have been possible; the instruments did not exist. Nor did the techniques for transmuting the understanding gained into commitment or the knowledge gained into action exist.

The best that was available was the due diligence, the Pre-Acquisition due diligence. That of course had been done and done well. But the best due diligence possible could, by custom and tradition, look only at certain factors. And these factors account for only about 20% of the success of a company—which of course accounts for so many disappointments in merger and acquisition work.

The other 80% is driven by the Operating Dynamic of the company. That complex of human and organizational factors that drives expectations, behavior, and results.

With Harry nudging, George and his team did look deeply in and saw what was really there. They did so in time to cause change before the damage went further.

Such clear vision, such intense drive to action, usually happens only in extreme financial crisis. But here all that had been anticipated. A virtual crisis had been created from the responses to The New Beginnings Survey©. A crisis that was safe for all the managers, but one that caused enough pain to generate the energy and the visceral commitment to change.

Reality, however uncomfortable, had been faced. Distaste at what they saw was felt and voiced. A new and better way of being, of relating to each other, of running the company was conceived, written, and committed to. Action was taken, right in that room for many things, and committed to in writing, before bosses, peers and subordinates. Action plans were put in writing for the things that had to wait.

They had addressed a hundred of the factors that drive performance. George and his team had identified problems with more than thirty. Five of these turned out to be GUT issues. Issues that were sucking the energy, drive, and creativity out of the company and out of its managers. Issues that had been growing, unseen, in the soul of the company. Issues that had to be dealt with, not just intellectually, but emotionally. Not just by the managers individually, but by the team as a whole, by the very company itself.

The issues were dealt with, just that way. Dealt with by George the CEO, by Alice the EVP of Sales, by the others individually, by the team acting together—by the company.

Then the day was done. Harry had his post-acquisition due diligence and knew now why his stomach had warned him. He patted it contentedly and in appreciation. In depth and in detail he had seen what was driving the company and each of its units. He had seen its strengths, he had seen its weaknesses. He had seen its innate trajectory—its very soul.

Of the things that needed fixing, many were already changed—simply by bringing them into the antiseptic sunlight of the session and making there, and documenting before all, the irreversible decisions that were needed. Others that would take more time were now detailed with specific action steps and dates that he would monitor and assist with. He held a copy in his hand.

The trajectory of the company, he knew, had changed.

The day was also done for George, his team, and his company. George, the team, and the company had had their New Beginning. They had seen in depth and in detail what was driving the company and each of its units. They had seen its strengths, had seen its weaknesses, its innate trajectory—its very soul.

Of the things that needed fixing, many were already changed; others that would take more time were now planned out and George would monitor progress and assist with them.

More than that, they were at peace—with Harry, with the holding company, with what was now expected of them.

Best of all, they were committed, both individually and as a team to their future—and they were moving.

The trajectory, they knew, had changed.

————————————————————————————————

Additional information on the Post-Acquisition Due Diligence can be found at: www.managementconsultants.com

Corporate Retrenchment or Corporate Renewal?

There are two major ways for managing officers to respond to downturn: one is to retrench, cut costs, pull back; the other is to renew, revitalize, grow stronger.

Strangely both responses look the same on the bottom line, at least at first: they both reduce costs. *But there is a profound difference in the long-term profitability and competitiveness of companies that renew, regenerate rather than just retrench.*

Retrenchment, even when it is done superbly, can produce a weaker, frightened organization that has lost muscle, market, bone, and spirit. Business literature and oral histories are full of ugly examples.

Renewal, though, that's different...

Corporate Retrenchment or Corporate Renewal?

The economy is in a slump. Corporate America's profits are plunging for the first time in years. The longest, most sustained economic growth in memory is now over. Many hope for an upswing soon, but just as many fear recession will stay with us, or something even worse. Business news is full of cutback talk and layoffs.

In this time of great economic distress there is a cry. The economy, the markets, the analysts, the investors and the boards are begging CEOs: "Do something! Do something now!"

Retrenchment, cutting costs, is typically the first reaction, and bringing costs in line with revenues is indeed seldom wrong. During the long upswing of business, costs grew unquestioned in many companies. Many unnecessary costs went unchecked—hidden by the flow of revenues.

So it is time, full time, for managers to act or at the very least react.

But there are two major ways for managing officers to respond to downturn: one is to retrench, cut costs, pull back; the other is to renew, revitalize, grow stronger. (There is of course a third way: do nothing and hope for the best—but let's not deal with that here. And this choice is always available.) Ah, the choice to make.

Strangely both responses look the same on the bottom line, at least at first: they both reduce costs. But they have a profoundly different effect on the long term profitability, competitiveness and potency (yes, potency!) of the company.

Retrenchment, at best, even when it is done superbly, merely leaves the company unimpaired. But retrenchment is rarely done that well. Done less than perfectly it produces a weaker, frightened organization that has lost muscle, market, bone and spirit. Business literature and oral histories are full of ugly examples.

Renewal, though—that's different. Though it always results in greater efficiency, at least as great as a 'cut-back' would achieve, its effects are positive. Leanness, agility, assertiveness, morale, strength, vigor are the terms that are used by those who experience it; not smallness, slowness, timidity or weakness, the connotations of retrenchment.

Renewal always gives a stronger company, aggressive, motivated and mobilized to command its future. Renewal gives a surge in profits, and always gives a leaner, fitter company. The savings that are realized are invested in its future or, in times like these, sent to its bottom line, for that ensures its future.

Renewal really means the reversal of the corporate aging process: a return to a younger, stronger state. Something that companies can do forever and, sadly, people cannot. The symptoms of retrenchment though are the symptoms also of age.

So, why do many managing officers choose retrenchment only, not renewal?

Many truly have not heard of Corporate Renewal, or think it just a nicer word for cut-back. Some really think it is not possible. Some think it something only charismatic leaders can achieve. Some think that turnaround or the return to profitability is the best that can be done. And many do not know how it is done. For it is never, taught in B Schools. And those who know and do seem never to be teachers.

Some are embarrassed, because the language of corporate renewal and regeneration is often thought of as unbefitting to business as if leadership and management were robotic exercises of intellect and not the mobilization of human heart and hope and will and vision. (How and when did business get the reputation of being a cerebral process?)

Also, in these past years of plenty, many managers were appointed who had never experienced the pinch of famine, who had never learned that it is possible to strengthen organizations in the face of diminished opportunities. Who had never learned that the very need for retrenchment brings with it an opportunity, the opportunity to renew.

So is renewal difficult?

Strangely, corporate renewal is easier and often quicker than retrenchment and, stranger still, costs less, always less. Strangest of all, it is most easily done when financial crisis or the economy can be cited as the reason. Renewal is in fact an innate and instinctive response of any organization to attack or adversity, but only when its leader can accept the challenge.

So, what should be done?

- If business conditions and good common sense say cut costs, then do so. But do it through renewal not retrenchment.
- If cutbacks have already happened and were done well, corporate renewal will provide more, still more savings.
- If cutbacks were done badly, then renewal is essential —if only to repair the damage.
- If cutbacks have yet to happen, then golden opportunity to renew, regenerate is there to take.

Are there things a CEO must know, must do?

Yes. Both "business" things and things that drive performance. The business things he knows already; they teach them in the B schools and discuss them every meeting of the board. The things that drive behavior, though, the factors that impel performance, these he innately knows as well. But they may be harder to articulate.

But there is a process that will work. And, because it is based entirely on human drives, on people things, it will evoke the very innate knowledge needed while it drives the decisions and the change.

How should that be done?

- First, the manager must throw down the gauntlet to his team and to his people, demanding a reinvigorated, leaner, more aggressive company, one altogether fitter and more dynamic than it now is. And give them hope. All leaders can do this— if they have confidence.

- Then his team must take the challenge and respond. Respond not just logically, in the intellect, but also viscerally, in the belly. Mobilize the emotional drives of the company. Muster its willingness to confront the challenges—and not just those of the economy, but also those of its soul, which are its real challenges. Evoke its willingness to sacrifice and collaborate and create. And finally, declare war upon the enemies of its survival: in its marketplace, like competitors; in its soul, like the cancers of ill will and lack of courage.

Is there a step-by-step process a CEO can undertake?

Yes, there is and well established too. It has been proven in the spirit and on the bottom lines of companies you know. Any manager can use it. It has just seven steps. Refer to the Preemptive Turnaround chapter for the discussion of these steps.

All that is needed is the courage to confront the deep issues of the organization and call upon the drive and commitment of its people. The process does the rest.

The Preemptive Turnaround

It has been known for decades that companies which turn-around from the brink of disaster (almost always under new management) experience a significant, sometimes abrupt, surge in profits. These turnaround companies revert to a younger more entrepreneurial stage—a rebirth takes place.

What is not well known, is that in subsidiary units of these turnaround companies, units that never were in trouble, even world class units, also experience the same surge, the same renewal. This happens while keeping the same management, but from strength rather than weakness, from ambition rather than desperation.

Research into these non need-driven, spontaneous surges, led to a unique process through which a CEO or managing officer can evoke a surge in profits, in competitiveness, in entrepreneurship, while reenergizing the organization and its management. The process, which evokes the fighting spirit of the company and its management teams, is uniquely effective. Here we look at the background, the approach, and the steps a CEO can take to trigger this "turnaround" response.

The Preemptive Turnaround
Renewing the Corporation:
Body, Soul and Bottom-Line

Fred's Tale

Fred is the president and founder. The firm writes small ticket leases—mostly automobile. He is a serious man, not prone to demonstrative behavior. Today he stands before his senior people— his direct reports and just a few others. Twelve in all. Thirteen with him. The number is unintentional, but he is conscious of its symbolism. They form the essential core of the company. Their relationships with each other, the dynamic of their interplay, cooperation and conflict, he thinks of as the company's driving spirit.

One year before, they had gone through a process that had left them strangely at peace. For the first time they—as a team, an entity—had seen and accepted the company exactly as it was—warts and all. They had seen themselves as they were too and accepted that. The process had been surprisingly easy and very quick. They had formed a safe place to do their work. And just did it!

They had gathered, consciously, as the core, the driving spirit of the company. For the very first time, through them, the company had seen itself as it truly was. The facts, the figures, those it knew already. It lived with them day-in, day-out. But its inner drives, its hidden motivations, its unspoken, unacknowledged attitudes, policies and politics—they were a revelation. Every manager may have known, but the company had not. The company had at last seen itself as it really was, and accepted that. It was at peace.

After that, it had to do something about what it had seen—about its problems, it potentials, its motivations—and it did. The managers had said of themselves and of the company, in almost these words: "This is who we are. God help us!" Then they had taken the energy they had released and invested it deep in corporate and personal commitments to a clear and simple picture of their future.

Fred is now going through the numbers. He says that they are not important—that the transformation in the life of the company is more important. But the numbers also tell a tale: one year later, month over month, revenues are up 110%!

THE SPONTANEOUS PROFIT SURGE

For 80 years it has been known that organizations that go right to the brink of disaster and then pull back—almost always under new management—experience a surge in profits, in performance, that can last two, three or even more years. Not only that, but by all measures, those turnaround companies revert to a younger, more competitive, more entrepreneurial stage of their corporate life cycle. A renewal and rebirth takes place. In the crisis of turnaround, something important within the organization is touched and changed.

What is not so well known is that, under the impetus of turnaround, units that never were in trouble—high performing, even world class units—also experience the same surge in performance, the same renewal, the same "turnaround". Just by being in the vicinity and sharing the same intense experience a renewal response is triggered. This response is derived from a place of strength rather than weakness, and from ambition rather than desperation.

Of course it is not feasible to revitalize a company by forcibly bringing it to the brink. In the discovery that strong high performing organizations can measurably surge in performance and experience a spontaneous "turnaround" with the same management and at essentially no cost, we found a clue to a buried treasure that exists within every company—the innate instinct to renew, to heal, to thrive.

THE TRIGGERS OF RENEWAL

During an actual crisis-driven turnaround a host of organizational drivers and behavioral triggers come into play, many of them unequivocally destructive. From our research into the "spontaneous" turnarounds we found that in these cases many fewer drivers are involved. Of these drivers (There are seventeen in all) four overwhelmingly dominate the process. They are:

- A profound simplification of politics;
- A palpable discharge of emotional energy, corporate as well as personal—Catharsis;
- An investment, and a deep commitment, of this same energy into a simple, clear, picture of the future of the company—Cathexis;
- Immediate action!

Finding a way to cause a company to create and to experience these drivers, especially the dominant four, became our challenge.

THE APPROACH

It took a while, mostly of trial and error, but eventually we succeeded. We created a simple and predictable approach and process that triggers the renewal response within healthy companies. This approach works for entire companies or units of companies.

The approach is based on truths that senior line managers know intuitively, but seldom talk about:

Every organization has an essential core, a corporate spirit. This spirit is not the CEO, though the CEO is and must be part of that core. It is not the corporate culture; it is something much, much greater.

When the essential core, the spirit, of a company is touched and changed, then the company changes. When the core of the company changes, its people want to change, its units want to thrive and grow. If reengineering needs to happen, its people cause it to happen. If a fundamental new attitude to selling is needed, then its people will adjust, willingly, even eagerly. (Well 80% of them.) If quality needs to improve, they will see to that too. Whatever is hurting the company will be brought to the surface and there, in the bright light of day, dealt with. Whatever is needed for the survival and success of the company will be brought out also—and obtained.

Under the right conditions, renewal happens very quickly and with almost no effort.

Renewal must be led by the managing officer. This does not need to involve a lot of time. At its simplest, the approach can be stated as:

A. Identify the essential core (or what is to be the essential core) of the company.

B. Have it recognize and acknowledge itself as the essential core.

C. Take this core through a process that will create within it the triggers/drivers of renewal: Simplification of Politics, Catharsis, Cathexis and Action!

This may sound too simple, but the reality turned out to be almost exactly that. The great complexity and expense of traditional corporate "improvement" programs from reengineering on back, often seems to be not really essential. They work from the outside in hoping that by changing the body the soul will change. Occasionally they work.

THE SPIRIT OF THE COMPANY

The spirit of the company—the essential core—resides primarily in the relationships between its senior managers. This is typically the CEO/managing officer, immediate reports and a few others, perhaps a dozen in all. The remainder resides in the subordinate teams. How they relate, how they view themselves as a group, and how they behave as an entity, shape the spirit of the company.

All it takes is that they see, acknowledge, and empower themselves as that core—then behave as one. It may be easier when there is a charismatic and inspired leader, but it will happen anyway under the right set of circumstances.

Fortunately, under the right stimulus, individuals instinctively form themselves into such entities. If they are the senior managers of an organization, they become its spirit.

So how do you get the managers to become the spirit of the company?

Frankly, by just talking with them collectively, as if they were already an entity. Expecting them to behave as an entity. Turning up the heat (more about that later) and having them/it face, battle, and decide about the real GUT issues of the company. It is that simple.

As the individual managers work the issues of the company in concert with their peers—they *become* the company's essential core, its spirit, its heart. Expecting them to act as the core, causing them to act as the core, brings that core into being and into awareness of itself. And makes it possible for the core to change itself.

How do you get the core to change? That is relatively simple too. The same stimulus and the same conditions that cause the essential core to come into being and into self awareness, will change it. It does not happen instantly, but it takes just hours.

For an individual to truly change is difficult, perhaps even impossible. Relationships however can change very easily.

Small events can sometimes drastically change relationships. Usually it is for the worse. But under the right kind of stimulus, under the right conditions and controls, it is easy for relationships between managers to change positively. As the spirit of the company resides primarily within the relationships of the senior managers, when their relationships change the core changes too and then the company changes.

So how do we provide the right stimulus and create the right circumstances? How do we get the company to create the drivers of renewal?

A financial crisis of course, can provide the discharge of energy—catharsis. But in a real crisis, with real danger, a huge amount of energy is released and does a huge amount of damage. It traumatizes the entire company. True, turnaround management can use some residual part of that energy to break barriers and change direction, but in practice they can use only a tiny fraction. All the rest works its way destructively through the organization. The condition of everyone being in a survival mode can provide the other three drivers: simplification, cathexis, and action. But not all crises have a happy ending.

THE PROCESS

It took us a long time to create the process. Research provided insight and the four key drivers were identified early. The process eventually required trial and error with scores of organizations.

The process turned out to be very straightforward. Only two people are needed to begin it. The first of course, is the CEO or the Managing Officer. It does not necessarily take a great deal of time but he must be involved as the initiator, periodically through the process, and as the final decision maker. Without his leadership and follow through nothing much happens. Charisma is optional.

The other needed person is an outside Catalyst—unless the CEO is brand new and has the right experience. The process works so quickly that "facilitator" is inadequate as a descriptor. He works intimately with the CEO: to identify the issues and drivers of the organization; to develop a plan of approach so that the managers can not slide off. He is seen as truly objective, is acknowledged as the counterbalance to the CEO's authority, and is a fierce advocate of the company's success. The qualities needed in a catalyst are:

1. Experience with many companies, our experience suggests more than 50;

2. Broad expertise in hard consulting projects across all functions of business;

3. Ability to handle group dynamics;

4. An instinct for transmuting a negative issue to a positive thrust, to the bottom-line;

5. Ability to fly with the corporate eagles—the management team.

There are just seven steps to the process:

Step 1. Put the senior managers in a room, those who are, or ought to be, the soul of the company. Create an emotionally safe place. Common sense will tell who the key players must be. The top dozen or so, usually. A CEO who is committed to making a safe place for all his managers and all points of view will find he has done so. In our work we find it useful to have in the room no desks or tables behind which people may hide emotionally. An arc of chairs works best, facing very large screens to display and record commitments. We use special software—MaxThink—for this.

Step 2. Cause the key players to identify both as a group and individually, at the emotional level, the real issues and motivators of the organization, particularly the GUT issues that suck the life energies from the company. Intellectual identification alone is not enough. Cause them to see and accept the company as it really is, and themselves as they really are. The CEO is allowed to acknowledge some limitations here. In case of perfection he can lie.

Step 3. Allow them to feel and express revulsion at each issue that they do not like. They must do this both individually and as a group. This is a lot easier than might be imagined. People do it instinctively, and it is never traumatic, though it might seem scary in anticipation.

Step 4. Create a catharsis on each issue. Cause the energies that have been bound up in these issues to be released. This is not difficult. People do it instinctively. If the issues are the real issues, if the group and the individuals do not slide off (so don't let them), the catharsis happens.

Step 5. Cause the energies to be transferred to, and invested in, an element of the CEO's and their vision of the future, immediately on the moment of catharsis—everyone will know it. In psychological terms the investment of energy and motivation into an idea is called cathexis. It happens in moments.

At first the elements will be just the antitheses of the issues. The energies coming from revulsion and going into their opposites. But as the elements accumulate, as they begin to form a picture (blueprint) of the future, the managers begin to see and especially feel the possibilities for them and their company.

A real enthusiasm, excitement, builds. New energy becomes available and gets invested into new increasingly ambitious elements of the blueprint. As the managing officer is leading, as the senior managers are invested, each element will make business sense—that is the acid test. The catalyst will see to this. The overall blueprint will have its feet in reality. Keeping the planning horizon down below three years helps too.

Without effort, intuitively, the business blueprint crystallizes around the vision of the CEO, even if it is unspoken, even if he is not there. Each manager adds strategies, tactics, detail, color, flavor—whatever he needs. Without thinking about it the managers buy-in at the emotional level. Under other circumstances this buy-in is the most difficult thing to get. Here it is easy.

Step 6. Have the managers commit to, viscerally, specific action steps to achieve every element of the blueprint. Record these so all can see. We use a special system to record and display, in real time, these action steps. They become on-line action plans.

These action steps must convince everyone in the room that they can produce the results needed. The drive and commitment of those who must perform the actions must be convincing too. Fortunately, very few people can lie convincingly under the close attention and interest of their boss (important), peers (more important) and subordinates (most important of all). So their commitment will be genuine

Step 7. Begin implementation immediately—that day wherever possible. The following business day at the latest. And follow up! Follow up! Follow up!

Of these seven steps, Step 2, identifying the true corporate issues is the only one that requires any preparation. There are a number of ways to achieve this from third party interviewing, to requests for suggestions, to open space planning, to round table discussion.

In our work, we use a special management questionnaire, The Corporate 360° Profile®. This shortens the process greatly. This instrument is given to all managers and supervisors ahead of time. It is answered anonymously. It addresses more than 150 factors that we have found from our experience with hundreds of organizations to underlie, cause or predict organizational performance. The instrument also elicits suggestions.

It is never possible to predict which of these many factors will be issues for any given organization, though some are found more often than others are. However, we have found that "good" companies—companies that are and have been consistently successful on the bottom line and in the marketplace—will find some thirty issues that the managers don't like, that are siphoning off energy or causing serious distress. An organization that has been experiencing difficulties for some time may find perhaps sixty issues.

These issues absolutely have to be dealt with, not just intellectually, but viscerally, emotionally, in the very soul and belly of the company, before serious transformation can happen. This can be a noisy and boisterous affair, but well worth while. It happens quickly and it's fun too.

THE RESULTS

In steps 3 through 6, (revulsion, catharsis, cathexis, action!) which occur over and over until all the serious issues are dealt with, a great number of things happen and a great many benefits accrue. The most tangible is the creation of a business blueprint and action steps that are deeply committed to by the managers. These, of course, are valuable by themselves. Housing them online makes them particularly useful. (You get an online strategic and operational plan through which you can drive and monitor every aspect of the business if you want it.)

The immediate surge in profits which we always find when the program has been undertaken fully, is also worthwhile. Greater than 20% in the first year is not uncommon. But the really important things happen within the spirit of the company. It is from these changes that the long term health and success of the company develops. The senior managers become a true team, the essential center of the company—its spirit. This spirit becomes aware and empowered. Centered on the CEO/managing officer, focused powerfully on the mission and blueprint of the organization, which it has created and committed to, energized into action, this spirit empowers the individual managers including the CEO, and holds them accountable.

Unexpected things, seemingly contradictory and apparently mutually exclusive things, happen too. The CEO becomes more empowered as a leader and also as a delegator. At the same time his immediate reports become more adaptable, more responsive to the CEO and also more empowered to contribute and be heard as part of the essential core. All become more willingly accountable. Within their own areas, their power to lead and delegate grows as well. All this is not magic. When the right environment is created, that which is wise within the company and that which is instinctive within people comes to the surface and is enhanced.

In processing the gut issues of the company at the emotional level the politics of the organization become simplified and clean. Energy, that has been bound up in unresolved, unacknowledged, even previously unknown issues is released and reapplied.

The relationships between the individual managers change too. A changed set of relationships changes the spirit of the company. A changed spirit transforms performance. A changed performance changes the bottom line.

Over the last several years we have been fortunate to observe numbers of companies who have undertaken this process and been allowed to track their performance over the following two years. Those who have undertaken the full program have all significantly transformed corporate attitudes and performance. The smallest first year profit increase we have recorded was 10%.

The only prerequisite for these companies to succeed was a CEO with the courage to look unflinchingly into the soul of his company and ask it to change—Body, Soul and Bottom Line.

Corporate Viagra®

An extraordinary similarity exists between corporate success and effectiveness and human male potency. Both are functions of psychology, vigor, energy, money, health, opportunity and age. For both man and company, an early sign of sickness, depression, fear or age is impotence—partial, intermittent or persistent.

In both cases, impotence is seldom discussed. In males shame and embarrassment are often at the root of its denial, but it is mostly ignored. Though the advent of Viagra® is causing the condition in males to be raised more often, it is still a source of embarrassment.

Corporate Impotence, especially the early stage, is the first indicator of deep-seated problems that will grow and fester in the darkness until brought to light by crisis—the economy turning down, the market or the industry or technology changing, someone internally making a mistake.

Corporate Impotence has many symptoms, many expressions, and many degrees of pathology. At its core is ineffectiveness, the inability to make things happen, the inability to cause events to take place in the company and the marketplace.

But there is an antidote...

Viagra® is a registered trademark of Pfizer Company

Corporate Viagra®
Do You Need It? Can You Get It? Is It Fun?

"FLACCID!!" *Alice, the only female board member snapped out suddenly* *"LIMP!"*

The chairman choked off his presentation mid-word, his eyes bulging, his throat constricting into a gurgle. The others froze, looking straight ahead, catching no one's eye.

"NOT UP TO IT ANYMORE!!" *Louder now. She slammed the table with her fist.*

Who was she referring to? Who was she taking to? Someone here? At her age... ? Who would..? Alice was glaring right at the chairman. Surely not Alice and Harry!

"IMPOTENT!!" *Her face, normally pale, was now flushed. A hank of her steel gray bun had sprung high on her head, impelled by her vigor. She was pointing right at him. Jab! Jab! Jab!* *"IMPOTENT! LIMP! FLACCID!"* *A ghastly smile flickered across his numb face. He couldn't seem to control his mouth. Words were squeezing from his lips. "Well!... he! ... ah!.. he! ... Alice... well, ah ... none of us, hm... are getting any ah... younger...er, ah..."*

"PSCHA!!" *Disgust oozed in her voice. They all cringed. Is there such a word? The chairman thought errantly, his mind still refusing to deal with this. The new director leafed through his papers, looking for a place to hide.* *"DON'T FLATTER YOURSELF!!"*, *she hissed. She was now impaling the report on the table with that sharp finger. They could see the yellow cover dent. Stab! Stab! Stab!* *"I'M TALKING ABOUT THE COMPANY!!"* *She grew quieter for a moment, breathing*

sharply through her nose, pushing her rampant gray hair back into place. "THE COMPANY! IT'S IMPOTENT!"

"It's a long time since I've seen any excitement in that company. Doesn't anyone want to penetrate a new market? God knows, this thing", she viciously stabbed the report again, "this thing, tells me there is a lot of market out there. And, let me tell YOU something, there's a lot of stiff competition out there doing something about it." Now she grew quiet, "Harry! This company is acting like it's in late middle age. It's only thirty-seven years old and ... and it can't hack it any more. Like some..." She pointedly refrained from finishing the rest of that sentence. The chairman steadfastly ignored a choking sound from somewhere to his left.

"If we don't DO something soon, the company is going to start dying. And the economy isn't helping either. " She paused a while. "What it needs, what it really needs", she was picking up speed again, "what the company really needs is a strong dose of VIAGRA®!"

———————————————————————

CORPORATE IMPOTENCE

All across the country, every month, directors and managers privately, quietly think such thoughts. Seldom voicing them and then only one-on-one. When they do, they use other images, other analogies. They never tell the CEO. The very person who should be the first to know is the last to be told.

Problems of drooping enthusiasm, softening drives, problems of corporate impotence, do exist. One way or another the problems must be addressed. As the likelihood of economic downturn grows, the urgency grows.

An extraordinary similarity exists between corporate and human male potency. Both are functions of psychology, vigor, energy, money, health, opportunity and age. For both man and company an early sign of sickness, depression, fear or age is impotence—partial, intermittent or persistent.

In both cases, impotence is seldom discussed. In males shame and embarrassment are often at the root of its denial, but it is mostly ignored. Though the recent advent of Viagra® is causing this condition in males to be raised more often, it is still a source of embarrassment.

In Corporate Impotence the reason for silence is blindness. This disorder has not received widespread recognition or a formal name, and often, even those most effected do not notice the condition. Companies, after all, seldom have partners who complain forcefully. Clients just quietly go elsewhere.

Once Corporate Impotence becomes late stage it will be noticed. But by then, the pathology is well advanced and impotence is overshadowed by other corporate diseases that are recognizable and have names. By the time everyone sees it, it is too late.

Corporate Impotence, especially the early stage, is the first indicator of deep-seated problems. Untreated problems will grow and fester in the darkness until brought to light by a crisis—the economy turning down, the market or the industry or technology changing, someone internally just making a mistake.

Corporate Impotence has many symptoms, many expressions, and many degrees of pathology. At its core is ineffectiveness, the inability to make things happen, and the inability to cause events to take place in the company and the marketplace.

In the early stages, symptoms can be intermittent, partial, and subtle and usually are explained away as something else. As the condition progresses the symptoms will become intense, constant and quiet unmistakable, and finally, inexcusable.

EARLY STAGE INDICATORS	LATE STAGE INDICATORS
Knowing What to Do, but Reluctant to do it	No Longer Knowing What to Do.
Lack of Enthusiasm	Apathy
Lack of Urgency	Weariness
Lack of Energy	Paralysis
Worry	Fear
Poor Execution	Persistent Quality Problems
Lack of Innovation	Resistance to Anything New
Reluctance to Argue	Backstabbing
Slow Decision Making	Paralysis or Capricious Decision Making
Tolerance of Mediocrity	Tolerance of Incompetence
Slowness to Adapt	Rigidity
Complacency	Denial and Terror
Poor Profitability	Loss

A few of the indicators or symptoms that we see quite often are shown above. For an even more comprehensive list just ask a middle manager casually what he thinks the symptoms of organizational ineffectiveness are. The presence of any or even all of the early-stage indicators is not definitive. Severity, duration, and a host of other factors also play a role. Sooner or later the early indicators turn into late stage symptoms. Even one symptom can be fatal, but you never find just one.

Two instruments can be used to take the guesswork out of early stage diagnosis. One is a short questionnaire for senior manager use to establish probable cause and make a preliminary diagnosis. The second is the Corporate Vitality Profile (CVP) which is quite extensive. The CVP addresses all the factors we mentioned above and many others. Some factors are obvious. Others are subtle. All are unique predictors/precursors of corporate impotence.

Every company has a unique vitality profile. Of the hundred plus factors the CVP addresses, we can never predict which will apply to any one company. What is known is that if early stage impotence is there, the company will show at least thirty symptoms. This CVP questionnaire has proven to be much more illuminating (and, of course, immensely more cost effective) then the most exhaustive interview of even all the senior management.

Such a comprehensive instrument as the CVP is used to enable management to prove conclusively to itself that the problem exists. Management, like individuals, can be unconsciously reluctant, even unwilling, to face uncomfortable and embarrassing realities unless there is overwhelming evidence and unless someone courageously holds the mirror. The comprehensive CVP is also used to define clearly and explicitly the underlying causes so that unambiguous and precise corrective actions can be taken.

In males, Viagra® works without improving the underlying physical conditions. It is a temporary relief of symptoms. The underlying problems continue to exist. The corporate equivalent works by healing the organization at a deep and central level. Its effect is not temporary—it is long term!

Corporate Viagra® works by renewing and revitalizing companies. It restores them to younger, healthier, more entrepreneurial, more aggressive, more creative, more potent states. It is quick. Results are evident in a matter of days. It is this renewal and regeneration that causes the surge in effectiveness and performance.

What is this Corporate Viagra®? It is a brief, intense process that is led by the CEO. This process, the Corporate Renewal Process, triggers an instinctive renewal response that is inherent in all organizations.

It has been known for more than eighty years that companies which "turnaround" from the brink of disaster, almost always under new management, undergo this innate renewal and revitalization response. They return to a younger more vibrant state. It shows almost immediately on their bottom lines.

What is not nearly so well known is that healthy, untroubled units within these companies, units which keep their management, also achieve the same inherent response, experience the same increase of potency and achieve the same, often better, profit surges. They do this from a position of strength rather than weakness, from ambition rather than desperation.

Our observation and research into this phenomenon led us to develop our Corporate Renewal Process. Simply put, these businesses had been touched and transformed at some fundamental level. Their very spirit, their essential core had been renewed and reignited. It was this renewed spirit that caused everything else to happen, and it happened almost effortlessly.

This is not the place for a philosophic discussion on the existence of the corporate spirit. (For a philosophic discussion refer to The Preemptive Turnaround and Fire in the Corporate Belly chapters for this.) For now, let us accept these facts. A company has a psyche, a spirit, an essential core. This spirit resides mostly in the relationships between the managers and the teams. Relationships under the right conditions can change easily. A change in spirit causes a change in the performance of the company. Many intuitive leaders feel these facts are axiomatic and behave accordingly.

Traditionally corporate transformations that retain existing management have relied on massive process and structural reengineering to work. These transformations cost a great deal in money and effort, take a long time, and are successful only a third of the time. But Corporate Viagra®, working directly with the spirit of the company, has no such limitations. Its success rate approaches one hundred percent.

For practical purposes it does not matter what constitutes the corporate spirit or where it is. What matters is that it can be addressed directly. Gather the CEO and the senior managers in a room and the spirit of the company is there. If this sounds mystical, hang in there. It may sound like magic and it may work like magic, but it is profoundly practical.

The senior managers are those who report directly to the CEO. They are those most responsible for conditions as they are. It is these senior managers who have to alter their behaviors if a corporate transformation is to happen.

Individuals find it difficult to change themselves in any significant way, at least not quickly, but under the right conditions relationships between people can change very easily and very quickly. Change relationships amongst managers at a deep level and the spirit changes. Change the corporate spirit and the performance of the company changes.

The Corporate Renewal Process because it triggers an instinctive response within a company is profoundly simple. The CEO/managing officer leads it. Senior management drives it and does all the work. While it is often best facilitated by a professional business catalyst who guides the process and triggers the changes, it can be done by the CEO.

Using the Corporate Renewal Process the CEO causes the essential core of the company to address frontally, and to reject cathartically the traits within that are causing the problems and to generate in their place the corporate attributes that are needed for corporate potency.

To begin the Corporate Renewal Process only one person needs to see and acknowledge the existence of corporate ineffectiveness and make the determination to begin. This person is the CEO or managing officer. Others may see the need, but unless the CEO commits nothing can happen. He must have the courage to start the process and lead his people. In fact, middle managers, who are first to see and complain (to each other) of the problem, are the last to volunteer to undertake the renewal process, to take their medicine. And, in a real sense, the renewal process is their medicine.

The process has just seven steps, transitions really. With the right intent and the right attitude on the part of the CEO, these transitions occur naturally.

1. The members of the management team (or what is supposed to be the management team) become in fact the spirit, the essential center of the company. The team becomes self-aware and believes in and acknowledges its authority as that spirit.

2. The management team, now a truly cohesive Team, sees and acknowledges the company as it is and themselves exactly as they are. They acknowledge the corporate and human (emotional) drivers of performance. They do this both as the spirit of the company and as individuals. The only preparation that is needed is the identification of the real issues that lie at the heart and belly of the organization and drive its performance. A comprehensive questionnaire, like the CVP, that addresses both the drivers of performance as well as the early warning signs of trouble is recommended.

3. The Team generates a real, visceral revulsion against those factors within the company that is causing the corporate impotence. Individuals share in this. A catharsis happens. Energy for change is released.

4. The Team defines for the company a new and detailed business blueprint. A blueprint that defines not just the usual strategies, tactics goals and objectives, but also defines and describes the spirit of the company.

5. From the energy of this catharsis, the Team creates within itself a powerful commitment to this new future described in the Blueprint. Detail by detail. Corporate and emotional driver by corporate and emotional driver.

6. With that same energy the Team commits both as the spirit of the company and as individuals to explicit actions to achieve each and every element of the business blueprint and to accept full accountability.

7. Implementation and follow-up begins immediately. No time is lost.

The mechanism is profoundly simple. The CEO and management team sit down and address the issues one by one. Address the issues not just intellectually, but also emotionally. As long as they do just three things, the rest will follow:

1. Confront all the real issues—even though they are embarrassing.
2. Keep in mind the transitions that are needed.
3. Demand direct bottom line impact from every thing that is committed to.

Results begin to show immediately. Initially the results are seen within the emotional life of the team and the company. Then, systemically, they appear on the bottom line.

The first result is a palpable sense of relief. This happens within the first couple of hours.

The second result is the simplification of the politics of the company; there are no more secrets. As that happens corporate success becomes the real goal of the team and its individual members. Other complicating politics vanish as inconsequential and trivial. Managers are now helping each other.

The third result is the birth of the team as an empowered entity that can address any issue of the company or its own members and, with authority, causes the issue to be resolved.

There is growing enthusiasm, as the team, individually and collectively, defines its future in terms that make sense. Few people are motivated by numbers and most business plans are expressed that way.

The managers and the teams accept accountability and the expectation of being held accountable. The managers know, not just intellectually but viscerally, that changes can and are being made. Decisions get made with increasing speed and things start happening. The company is potent again.

Many, many more things also happen that depend on the unique condition and state of each company. Performance grows as things happen and are translated into actions that have positive bottom line impact. Often it surges.

The bottom line results that we have seen from this Corporate Renewal Process have been consistent, always significant and sometimes remarkable ranging into the millions of dollars. It appears that once the process is wholeheartedly driven by the CEO, it cannot fail to have the most positive results on the emotional life of the company, on its effectiveness, and on its performance.

While "Corporate Impotence" is not a term that is often used, every manager knows exactly what it feels like. Knows exactly its consequence to both company and people.

What has not been well understood is that there exists a Corporate Viagra®, a process of corporate renewal and revitalization that can be taken for this condition. It works rapidly and well. It works not only for companies in difficulties, but also works even better for companies that are healthy.

The only requirement for it to work is a CEO with the courage to make his managers look deep into the spirit of their company. And not run away.

Viagra® is a registered trademark of Pfizer Laboratories

Interview with a CEO

This interview was conducted by Terry Sullivan, then Executive Director of a major Chicago metropolitan business association.

Mr. Sullivan currently is a popular and successful writer whose work appears in many publications internationally. He is a regular contributor to GQ, Chicago Magazine, and the Chicago Tribune Sunday Magazine.

The person interviewed was Andy Mayo, the CEO of a member company who was also a board member of the association. He had first undertaken the corporate renewal process four years prior to this interview.

The interview covers the diagnostic instruments, the process, the style of the process, and especially the results, bottom line and otherwise. Examples are included.

Interview With a CEO
A Corporate Renewal Experience

A member of our board, Andy Mayo (AM) led his company through a remarkable performance improvement program a few years ago, the results of which are now well established. I thought his experience might be of interest to our CEO members.

As many of you have remarked during our round table discussions, the single most difficult task in an established company, is its renewal. Sometimes it is called revitalization, sometimes shot-in-the-arm, sometimes turnaround. Many companies, maybe all, need it eventually. Maybe once a decade in good times and in times of high change, like now, more often.

Over the last 30 years, a number of transformation processes have arisen: from Strategic Planning to MBO; from OD to Outward Bound; from TQM to re-engineering. Each one was promising to be the magic answer. In turn, each has waned, when it is realized the success rate is just 30% at best; more likely 20%; and maybe success was caused by something else anyway.

Andy underwent a process that has been used in the Chicago area since at least 1986. It has a success rate measured on the bottom line of nearly 100%. It uses a simple, common sense, process and achieves significant results. I thought an interview with Andy might be interesting.

RESULTS

Terry Sullivan (TS): Andy, thanks for taking the time for this interview. To cut right to the chase, what were your results?

AM: To summarize the results, in terms of bottom line: on revenues of $6 million we increased our profits by almost $1 million, within one year. Most of the results came in the first eight or nine months.

TS: Where did those profits come from?

AM: Mostly from efficiency improvements. We did not focus on sales growth at that time. Later we did the program again and pushed the revenue side. It looks now as if this year will be a record year for sales.

TS: What other results did you see?

AM: There were a lot really. I think the first thing I noticed was how much more responsive the company was to my management. Then morale was better, almost right away. A lot of the repressiveness that was traditional to our industry had dissolved during the sessions and that was a great help. People who had felt themselves to be powerless now felt empowered.

People began to identify problem areas on their own and fixed them or ask that they be fixed. A lot of internal blocks got dealt with that way.

Communications were much, much better. When communication is really good you don't need so much of it. The initial honest communication happened at the sessions and we kept it up.

The culture was opened up so we could look at ourselves in the eye more easily, ask objective questions and decide what needed to be done.

Some people who were not successful in the old culture were able to flourish in the new.

We really saw the changes in us when we did the questionnaire again a couple of years later. Boy, were we different.

THE PROCESS

TS: How does the program work?

AM: It allows a company to discover and deal with the real issues that are driving its performance. This sounds simple, but in fact it is the most difficult part of any revitalization program. Management sees a problem, even acknowledges it, but then somehow does not deal with it or only partially deals with it. It is too emotionally difficult. This program does not let us avoid the problems. It allows management to see what is going on in the company, why it is behaving that way, and then actually do something about it.

Also, other levels of the company bring up issues that management has not seen as significant and the process establishes their true importance in the cold light of day, and then do something about them. Staff love that. Managers too, after the first shock.

TS: What kinds of things does it bring out?

AM: It is a very comprehensive process. It is designed to bring up whatever needs to be brought up. This is different for every organization. In our case it surfaced operational issues, cultural issues, people issues, strategic issues and tactical issues.

A few examples: I realized we had been living in a fools paradise as to how our clients viewed us; operations that I thought were OK turned out to be in need of major overhaul; Morale! Well I don't want to talk about what that was. We found scores of issues, some major, some minor, and then we did something about them. You see, that is what is really different about this program. You actually do something about your issues, and everybody in the company helps.

Let me give you a people issue example. Our secretaries were a major cause of discontent and operational problems. I had heard grumbling before, but when we saw and appreciated just how serious it was, we did something. Morale must have gone up 20 points on that alone, and the operational improvements that permitted proved to be a big piece of the profit improvement I mentioned earlier.

TS: Can you give me a strategy example?

AM: Yes. This one was a major turning point for us: when we put all our answers together and talked about them, openly, it became clear that the business we were in was deep in change. We were not. We had to make a major shift in strategy, instantly. We did. We had to get out of the custodial business and we had to make our business profitable. That had beneficial, long-term consequences.

An operational example was the realization that our billing process was much less than it should be. This was uncomfortable news for some of us, but we faced it anyway. That led to another big piece of the profit improvement. There was a lot of facing the truth in the program.

TS: What can you tell me about the process?

AM: In one way it's very simple. We answered a questionnaire, anonymously. The management team then analyzed their own and their subordinates answers. Then, while we were doing that, the team committed to a detailed blueprint of where they wanted the business to be, and how it was to behave, in a couple of years. Each person committed to specific, verifiable actions that are designed to correct the problems and to fulfill every element of the business blueprint. Those action steps were monitored and followed up.

Of course all that is just the surface. The commitment, drive and energy raised during the process is what causes real changes to happen and become permanent. That's hard to describe.

TS: Talk some more about the questionnaire.

AM: It is usually given only to managers and supervisors. But, because of the highly complex nature of our work with our clients, we gave it to all our staff. It was quite large, but it took only about an hour to fill out. It asked some very unexpected questions about things I would not have thought were important, but they were. Also it asked what seemed to be dull questions about the competition, corporate style, management behaviors and such, but when we saw our answers, then they were very interesting. I think it measured about a hundred factors. Only six or seven proved to be of major importance to us, but a bunch more had to be dealt with too.

TS: How was the questionnaire processed?

AM: The consultants did not digest the answers for us. They computerized the responses, but they made us analyze them ourselves. Where it was right for us to get upset about our answers, they made us do that, too. They would not let us hide from our answers. They referred to it as "holding the mirror", until we had really seen ourselves for what we were, warts and all, and finally admitted it. It is an extraordinary process. Most of it happens in the belly rather than the head.

TS: Can you remember any of the answers now?

AM: No. At the time I thought I would never forget. What was important was they were the truth, and we had to admit it because we had said it, not some outsider. Some of it was painful. Maybe that's why I don't remember, but I do remember that the next time we did the questionnaire, the answers were better and so was our bottom line. Those answers turned out to be the Leading Performance Indicators for our business.

TS: After you answered the questionnaire, what did you do?

AM: The management team went to a conference center for the initial sessions. When I went in the first morning, I thought we were in the wrong room. There were no tables, just a line of chairs facing overhead projector screens with computers attached.

We dealt with each issue as it arose. We defined action steps to fix them. We created new goals and then specified action steps to achieve the goals. Then we took action after action until the goals were achieved one inch at a time.

Of course I know that that does not tell you anything of the changes in the culture and behavior of the management teams and in the way people worked together. The results really came from all of that.

After the senior team did their work, we led the next levels of the organization through it. Eventually, everyone took responsibility for implementing the future. They defined and accepted action steps to achieve things and were measured on their accomplishment.

OTHER RENEWAL PROGRAMS

TS: You mentioned that you created action plans as part of the process. How is what you did different from planning?

AM: The purpose of planning is to create a plan. What we did was transform our bottom-line and competitiveness. The plan was just something we used to capture the commitments made and to follow up with, but technically you could call it planning. One of my senior managers evaluated what we did against strategic planning guidelines put out by one of the big six accounting firms and found it met all those criteria, and then some.

Over the years we have done a lot of strategic planning, but I never experienced any significant profit increases because of it. In fact, I read recently that strategic planning has never been associated with significant profit increases, but the results of the program we undertook were entirely different from any planning I had ever done before. Also, the style and pace of it were about as different as you would get. But the term "planning" has a soothing ring to it and I think we referred to it as planning when we first introduced it to the staff.

RE-ENGINEERING

TS: How does it compare to Business Process Re-Engineering?

AM: As a result of the program we did very significant re-engineering of our organization: structure, process, systems, everything. The program really re-engineered our soul and it gave us the commitment at every level to do a complete reengineering job. The low success rate of traditional reengineering programs is due to the lack of this commitment. You could say that the program was the front-end of our reengineering.

DURATION

TS: How long did the program take?

AM: Well the senior team went through it in four days: Two days the first week and two days the next. I think 90% of all the hard work and corporate decision-making were done then. Subordinate groups took just two days each. The time it takes is a function of the size and complexity of the organization and how many people undertake it. Often, I believe, it is just the officers, managers and supervisors. We had everyone go through. For us that was right.

TS: When did you first see results?

As I look back, I think I began to see shifts in behavior and cooperation almost from the first day, right in the sessions. This resulted in *systemic* improvements across the board and we saw bottom line shifts within sixty days. Most of the results happened for us within eight or nine months.

CORPORATE MOTIVATIONS

TS: You described the process as one that engaged the emotions of the people. Can you describe how you felt during the process?

AM: A bit nervous at first, but there was never a feeling that things were out of control. Within a few hours we were relieved that the issues were out in the open and then jubilation that they were behind us. Morale was up. Especially mine!

I went away more empowered, more in charge of the company than when I went in. Interestingly all the managers felt they were more empowered, more supported.

TS: Did you have to change yourself much?

AM: To be honest, no, but I had to show I was willing to change. That was the most difficult bit in anticipation, but not in practice. What my people wanted me to do, by and large, was what I wanted to do for them. I'm told this realization is almost universal.

SELECTION OF CONSULTANT

TS: Why did you select the consultants?

AM: They were "strongly suggested" to us by our chairman. He knew of work they had done with a much larger company that had resulted in serious improvements and he hoped for the same with us. I wanted that too.

TS: How would you characterize the consultants.

AM: Well, they call themselves catalysts rather than facilitators. I agree with that. The program is much too energetic for mere facilitation. They say they are in the business of early decline or preemptive turnaround and they act as intervenors. But mostly I think of them as fiercely partisan on the side of the company. They are the advocates of the company's potential, and they will brave anyone, the CEO, managers, the workers, to represent that. The results we got were in great part because of this advocacy.

They were also very experienced. The lead catalyst at the time had consulted with more than 100 organizations in almost every conceivable area. The catalyst on second chair was equally experienced. He had run the financial services consulting practice for one of the Big 8 CPA firms in the Midwest for some years. They knew when people were waffling. They also knew what actions should be taken to bring the greatest results, and they would not accept promises or actions that did not have the real visceral commitment and emotional investment of managers. They were tough.

FOLLOW UP

TS: What kind of follow up did you do after the program was over?

AM: A major focus of the process is the creation of a detailed, step-by-step, action plan to achieve the goals we set. This is done by us during the sessions. It is put on our LAN so that we can follow up. This was particularly important in the months immediately after the process when we might have "forgotten" some of the harder things.

DOWNSIDE

TS: To everything there is a downside. What was the downside to the program?

AM: For me it was not being able to avoid dealing with the results of some decisions I had made. An example: I had appointed a very competent professional to a management role where he was not doing well. I was a bit defensive about that and my instincts were to avoid the issue, but I had to deal with it. Now I have another manager in that slot, a much more productive staff, and a successful and satisfied professional contributing to the company's future.

LIMITATION OF THE PROCESS

TS: What are the limitations of the process?

AM: The consultants did not tell us what to do. We had to make the hard decisions ourselves. We had to generate the commitment to actually implement them as well, though they acted as guides and sounding boards in the process, but in retrospect I think that probably was a strength, although I know that some organizations prefer an outside authority to come in and tell them what to be and what to do.

This program is based on the premise that the best place to find insight, direction, commitment and implementation is within the company itself. If you get those, then your people learn and the benefits are permanent. That has been our experience.

WHEN THE PROCESS IS MOST USEFUL

TS: At what stage in a business would this be most useful?

AM: Well the catalysts say that only about one-third of their clients are what might be described as "experiencing difficulties". We might have been in that category the first time we used them, though our profits were stable. Two-thirds of their clients range from average to high performers. I like to think of us as in the latter category the last couple of time we did the program, but the critical factor in the whole process is the readiness of the CEO. The consultants say that all that is needed is a managing officer with self-confidence and the desire to succeed. The process does the rest.

Hitting the Ground Running as the New CEO

In just two days it took two years off my learning curve. In just two days more it had allowed my new management team to imprint, really imprint, on me as their leader.

"I" was the new, the brand new, managing officer of a 1500 person company. "They" were my new team. Ten senior managers, all my age or older, with an average tenure of twenty years with the company.

I had had no say over who "they" would be; I had inherited them; They had no say over my arrival either; I had been appointed. Some of them, I'd heard, had applied for the position too.

"It" was a program of Corporate Renewal/Revitalization that had begun the day I was appointed.

As I looked at the results, I realized that I was looking into areas far beyond the usual financials and operating metrics, into the root causes of performance, into the very drivers of behaviors that were generating the performance.

"I knew what to change and how to change it."

                    Managing Officer - 1500 person company.

Hitting the Ground Running as the New CEO

HARRY

In just two days it took two years off my learning curve. In just two days more it had allowed my new management team to imprint, really imprint, on me as their leader. And, in a way I would never have dreamed possible, it had allowed me to commit to them as the managers I wanted and would create the future with.

"I" was the new, the brand new, managing officer of a 1500 person company. "They" were my new team. Ten senior managers with an average tenure of twenty years with the company.

I had no say over who "they" would be; I had inherited them; they had no say over my arrival either; I had been appointed. Some of them, I'd heard, had applied for the position too.

"It" was a program of corporate renewal/revitalization that by chance had begun the day I was appointed.

Before I go further, let me tell you a little about me:

I have been in business for 20 years, across many elements of the business from design to production, to supply chain, to distribution as engineer, supervisor, manager, and now CEO.

By formal education I am an engineer with an MBA.

I had worked in many other challenging positions, but not one as challenging as this, and never before with so many people reporting to me, depending on me.

From my point of view the program began with an email from my chairman announcing the survey. It informed me, and all the managers and supervisors in my new organization, that "to help with the planning process" (that sounded innocuous enough) we should go to a certain web address and respond to the survey to be found there; that we should do it within the week. I was given a password specific to the group I was answering with—in my case the senior team. Each of my managers and supervisors was also given a password appropriate to the group they were part of.

The survey was large. But with the questions phrased as statements and buttons to click on by way of response, it took me only about 35 minutes to complete. But I was left with a feeling that a number of the areas covered were unusual: I had filled out many surveys in my time, but there were many issues addressed here that I had not seen before. And I began to wonder what the answers of my new subordinates would show. And the answers of their subordinates, too. And what might the responses to the item "Our need for consensus gets in the way of needed decisions" imply about us?

There were a couple of weeks to wait. Then my boss called me and said, "Can you come and look at this?" I was about to get a private heads-up on the findings.

I knew there were a lot of challenges before I accepted the job. I had looked at some of the metrics of their performance and saw the signs. I also heard what it was like there from others I had worked with over the years, what some of the issues were, largely related to people, process and performance. I had been asked a number of times if I knew what I was getting into. I thought I did.

Now with the results so simply displayed, I saw the depth and pervasiveness of our problems. My chairman was saddened too, and he is an optimist. Why the *Consensus* question was included was now clear. And the questions on *Decision Making* and *Risk Taking* and *Acknowledgement of Performance* and even the one on *Tolerance of Incompetence*.

There were problems. There were indeed.

As my chairman and I looked at the results, we realized that we were looking into areas far beyond the usual financials and beyond the operating metrics and warning signs, into the root causes of performance, into the very drivers of behaviors that were generating the performance—into the very operating dynamic of the company.

There must have been a hundred questions, a hundred sets of responses, that showed an unhealthy workplace, where problems existed within and across groups. Problems which appeared to have festered a long time in the soul of the organization. Problems, that if left unaddressed head on, would continue to linger and plague future results as they had the past.

At the time I felt overwhelmed by the results: there were too many problems, too many areas out of balance, too many things to be fixed in the soul of the company. Because that is what we were talking about, fixing the soul of the company

But as we talked to the consultants who had designed the survey, it became clear that the results, the insights, the opinions of the respondents, like beams of light, were focusing on a few key issues, from different perspectives, from different levels of the organization.

And that these issues were really caused by that single corporate frailty all heavily regulated utilities are prone to: creeping bureaucracy. Except, in our case, it had long since stopped creeping and now had us in a stranglehold.

TOM

We did not design our program just for Harry. We did not design it to bring new CEOs instantly up to speed either. Though that is what it does and that is now a significant part of what we do.

The program was initially designed to turnaround troubled companies—preferably before the full financial crisis hit. At the time we called it Preemptive Turnaround. It worked, like a charm—on the bottom line where it could be measured.

We soon found ourselves using it further and further upstream of financial crises until the terms Turnaround, or Preemptive Turnaround no longer applied and Corporate Renewal or Profit Improvement were the better terms. Its impact on the bottom line was even greater.

The closer a declining company is to a financial crisis, the more technically difficult is the solution; the EXTERNAL players, like bankers, vendors, customers, investors, are not very willing to cooperate. If they do cooperate a heavy price will be extracted.

By the same token however, the closer the crisis is the more willing the INTERNAL players are to do what is needed.

The further a declining company is from a financial crisis the easier it is, technically, to fix its problems. Banks, creditors, investors, will all cooperate.

But the further the company is, or appears to be, from financial crisis the more difficult it is for the internal players to actually do anything about it. Management knows just what to do or can easily find out, but all too often an apathy, a paralysis, a corporate trance has taken hold.

This is the paradox of corporate renewal. It is also the greatest frustration of managers who want to make serious change.

What our process does is shatter the corporate trance. We designed it specifically for that. It causes a crisis, actually a *virtual* crisis, within the company. But unlike a real crisis, which destroys morale and productivity at every level, this virtual crisis is focused on and confined to the managers and supervisors who must break the pattern of decline and change the trajectory of performance.

This virtual crisis is without danger. The company cannot be hurt by it. But it is not without intensity and it causes all the soul searching and honesty a real crisis does. It has all the focusing power of a real crisis in which people can lose their livelihoods and reputations.

A business turnaround that is driven by a real financial crisis has just three major elements:

1.   **Catharsis**—In which management experiences an emotional revulsion with the way things are, the way the company performs, and the way its management and its people behave. This generates a huge amount of energy though most of it plays out destructively throughout the organization among people who have no power to initiate change.

2.   **Cathexis**—In which management (often a new management) invests, commits viscerally, the energy released by catharsis into a new vision, a new way of doing business, a new way of relating to each other and the marketplace. A new operating dynamic.

3.   **Action! Action!! Action!!!**—Immediate, sustained, and followed up.

Our process does this.

What is different is that we generate the motivation to change without the danger. We also work with *existing* management.

The creation of the motivation, the drive to change, is our first task.

To do this we use the knowledge, perspective, insight and honesty of the managers, the supervisors, the very people most stuck, most enthralled, most frustrated by the corporate trance. The very people who must initiate and lead the change.

To elicit this motivation we use a questionnaire—the Corporate 360°.

This survey primarily addresses the Drivers of Performance. These are the factors that underlie and impel the behaviors of the company. There are about a hundred of these factors. (The best known of these is perhaps MORALE. But in fact it is not one of the more significant drivers. It is much more a symptom.)

Together these drivers provide an in-depth, comprehensive profile of the operating dynamic of the company. This is what we use to drive the renewal of our client companies.

If we had not seen results like these before, we might have despaired. Certainly they were depressing. The issues were pervasive, through all levels of the organization. We were looking at *systemic* problems, not localized troubles. In fact, if it were possible for a company to be clinically depressed this one would be.

But we had seen it before. It was a pattern we had found in other heavily regulated companies. Fortunately it had within it the seeds of its own correction.

For Harry's organization there were about a dozen core issues, of which the top three were:

- Corporate Decisiveness,
- Acknowledgement of Performance, and
- Leadership.

We knew from experience that when these and the other key issues change, the company changes.

But something else had to happen first: Harry had to become the leader of his organization, not just the manager, not just on paper, but also in the eyes of his managers and their subordinates. He did not have much time. Without strong, accepted leadership at his level there could be no change

HARRY

The responses were depressing, but here and there in the questions and in the answers I began to see the first faint glimmers of hope. I felt that as I shared the responses with all my managers and supervisors things would change.

But then I knew that just sharing results would not be enough; a number of things would have to happen before knowing what we were would change the company into what we could be, should be.

First I would need to become, in full reality, the *leader* of my new organization.

Then the rest could happen. Then each member of my team and each member of their teams would be able to confront— and, I hoped, accept—what the organization was, openly, honestly, without flinching away. And feel the shame, the anger that would bring—because shame and anger *should* be felt at what I was looking at.

Then they would have to invest their emotional commitment into becoming something else. What that something else should be was already obvious.

Then they would have to take action, do it. I would, too, but their actions were going to be needed much more.

GETTING TO KNOW THEM

From my experience I had known just how long it takes to get your hands around a new organization. It is not the strategies, tactics or domain knowledge, however new, that are the challenge. It is the people. The management people, the supervisory people. The ones who make things work out there on the line.

Getting to know them always takes time. The more managers, the more supervisors, the more teams there are, the longer it takes. Getting their acceptance, of course, is something else. And getting them to imprint on the new leader, actually joining the team, something else still. I had heard too many stories of leaders who had found out too late what exactly they had inherited, or had taken too long to really take charge, or who had not obtained the loyalties of their teams.

I had been told we had little time. I had said I'd take the job. And there was still the catharsis, and the cathexis, and the action steps still to be taken.

But it turned out that they could happen together; it was to be part of the program we had contracted for. The diagnostic was just the first step.

THE PROCESS

The process has just two phases: 1) The diagnostic and 2) the Renewal sessions (In my case these were also the means of my investiture and assumption of leadership.)

The diagnostic was done, now it was time for the sessions.

It began with me and my new senior team meeting off-site. My chairman opened the session and then left us to the tender mercies of the consultants. We found ourselves sitting in an open arc of chairs, no tables to hide behind, looking at two large screens on which our answers and our subordinate's answers appeared.

But these answers appeared in a format very different from any survey results we had ever seen: there were no summaries, no charts, no scattergrams or averages or medians. Just our responses: 1, 2, 3, 4, or 5. We could see them all, and each of us privately knew where our own answers lay, and could compare them to our peers and to our subordinates.

The process of dealing with the answers was different too—as was the style. And that defies description. One has to experience it—because it was designed to trigger not just analysis and thought, but feelings, real feelings, revulsion where that was proper. And above all, commitments. Always commitments from the heart and the belly. And always turned into actions.

The questioning began. At first it was the consultants asking, but very soon we all caught the simplicity of them and asked them of ourselves and each other:

—What is the real answer here? (No, never mind the average, what's the REAL answer?)
—How do you feel about that? Really FEEL?
—What should it be? What will you COMMIT to making it?
—What is the action? Who will do it? When?
—Who will check to see it's done? To see it had the results we need?
—Who will defend and support the doers? That was often to be me. Defending the drivers of change is the role of leaders.

Then little by little, hidden in the questions and the answers and the laughter—there was a lot of that—the feelings of the people about the company began to shift. Their attitudes towards each other shifted. Their relationships with each other changed. Their relationships with me changed. They became a team. And I found myself, without ever having thought about it, committed to them as my team, my people.

Commitment after commitment, action after action, was recorded before our eyes. We had created an action plan to change our organization. Each of us had tens of actions to be taken, and we knew we would deliver.

Then the session was nearly over. It had taken two days. And we were very tired.

My chairman dropped in to see what we had wrought and watched my people pledge to me—and challenge me to support them. He watched me pledge to them. And then pledge to him the many, many actions I had committed to—by then I had more than forty and the list would grow thereafter.

Then he pledged to them and me, taking specific action steps for himself. And my people listened to what he said, and more importantly how he said it. Gauging clearly his commitment.

I went through the process fourteen times over the next couple of months—once with each of my direct reports and their teams, the supervisors. More insights, more relationships, more commitments to each other and more action items. In those two months, I saved years of slowly trying to understand the organization, the people and the issues. It was a leap start, which would move us forward very rapidly. Then we began to work, to implement our plans, to change our company.

TOM

Even after twenty years of doing what we do, it is still difficult to describe it to those who have not experienced it. Certainly the techniques we use, the questions we ask, the things we record are all simple enough. We have made them public. But the techniques alone do not account for the changes we see. They do not solely account for the results our clients achieve. A transformation takes place within the spirit of the company that allows its managers to transcend themselves.

For the changes seen here, these results are not ours. They are way beyond anything we might have contemplated. They are uniquely those of the company and the people who generate them: the responses to the questions are theirs; the analyses are theirs; the reactions (and sometimes the revulsions) are theirs; the commitment to change is theirs; the ideas are theirs; the plans are theirs; the actions are theirs; the achievements are theirs.

All we do is act as catalysts.

From time to time we issue follow up questionnaires so that the people and the company can see what progress is being made (long before the financials show) and tie the changes in the drivers of performance back to the changes in financial performance.

HARRY

Follow up after follow up, I watched the attributes of our organization change: first from apathy to purpose, then from uncertainty to decisiveness; and then from "management by exception" to generous acknowledgement, praise and guidance and, where needed, correction.

Time after time, I saw evidence the vision I had for the future become internalized, clearer and more certain, picked up in the hearts of our managers and supervisors.

And month after month, quarter after quarter the financials showed that progress too, and I knew why.

But also in that time I saw the occasional slippage here, back sliding there. Through the follow up surveys I knew why and what to do about it. Much more importantly, my managers new why, and what to do—and did it. And managers who might just not have made it in other circumstances, become high performers.

Since then, another challenge has been presented, another organization given to me. And once again they did not much like it, my new team. And once again the questionnaire goes out. And once again the results come in and show just how bad, and good, things are. And what must be done by me and my new team to fix it.

Harry ––– is a real person. Because of his company's publication policies, he wishes to remain anonymous.

From Politics to Purpose

No trade association executive, no chairman of the board, need be told that boards and politics go together; it is part of the human condition. A certain amount of politics is necessary for anything to get done.

But, politics is something that has an innate tendency to grow and flourish, like weeds, in numbers of issues, in complexity, in intensity.

Beyond some limited amount, an increase in board politics causes a deterioration of leadership

Left unchecked, the situation within the association progresses from distracting the board, to consuming the executive, to burning out the staff, then to missed opportunities, to mistakes, to gross errors, and so on.

However, progress down this path is not inevitable. Executives and boards can take action to halt it, even reverse it; from dissonance, back to harmony, even to the original resonance.

A process exists that executives and boards can use to profoundly simplify politics, and refocus the energies released by this into a renewal of purpose and leadership and a deep commitment to achievement.

From Politics to Purpose
The Rebirth of A Board

Harry's Story

I'm Harry. I'm the Executive Director....

It was over. The last meeting of the old era. By some alchemy it had also been the first meeting of the new. The chair declared the board meeting over, but nobody left. They should be tired, but they talked to each other instead of running away; they used to do that.

They were seeing each other differently and finding something good to say and praise and plan. Involving the staff, too. Alice, the new director, was now a veteran. They were no longer trying to suck me into their plots. It felt sooo good. The chair gave me a wink. They were treating me as one of them. Again.

Though they had not noticed it at the time, over the last couple of days we had been clearing the plaque out of the association arteries. Item by item. Issue by issue. Hard feelings, sulks, enmities too.

The chair had called it strategic planning. Alice, with her fresh eyes, knew it was corporate renewal. Later, we would refer to it as The Time of Spring Cleaning. There was a new beginning. A new energy. A new era was underway.

No association executive, no chairman of the board, need be told that boards and politics go together; it is part of the human condition—a certain amount of politics is necessary for anything to get done.

But, politics is something that has an innate need to grow and flourish, like weeds, in number, in complexity, in intensity. Beyond some limited amount, an increase in board politics causes a deterioration in leadership. It is as if politics feasts upon the finite energy of the board (and the staff).

Left unchecked, the situation within the association degenerates from distracting the board, to consuming the executive, to burning out the staff, and then to missed opportunities, to mistakes, to gross errors, and so on.

However, progress down this path is not inevitable. Executives and boards can take action to halt it, reverse it; from dissonance, back to harmony, even to resonance.

In the early stages this reversal is almost easy, if the signs and symptoms are seen and understood. But as conditions worsen, as the executive and senior staff are sucked deeper into the mire and become seen as part of the problem, it is harder. Eventually, executives must look to survival; board leaders to draconian measures.

A process exists that executives and boards can use at any time to profoundly simplify politics and refocus the energies released by this into a renewal of purpose and leadership and a real commitment to achievement. The process works, not just for early stage turnaround, but even for extreme cases.

The process, at its simplest, has just three components:

1. **Illumination:** Bringing to the surface the real issues, the secrets, and the demons of the organization. Depending on the level of politics, these can be many or few, severe or mild. There may be strategic, financial or operational issues among them. But always they will have personalities and person-to-person relationships at their root.

2. **Catharsis:** Causing the board (and staff if needed) to deal with these issues until they are resolved. All the issues of the organization must be dealt with eventually, but the core issues, the gut issues, the people and relationship issues must be dealt with first.

3. **Commitment:** Transferring the energies released into a gut commitment to a new future, a new behavior, and a new level of performance.

Harry's Story

One night a few weeks before, the chairman and I got together over beer to tailor the questionnaire. I contributed the probing questions about the board. He provided the questions about operations. Then, at a special meeting, the board and senior staff answered it. Anonymously. And why not! After all, we were going to be planning.

The whole association, body, soul, and bottom line would be lit from within, even to its darkest corners, its ghosts, its monsters.

This all sounds easier said than done. How, for instance, do you get them to agree to do it in the first place? How do you get at the real issues? How is an executive to do this without making mortal enemies? How can a chairman take on friends of many years? How do you make them talk? Change? It is simple.

LET'S DO IT!

Not by chance, the renewal process is also a planning process. Granted, it is a planning process that addresses more than the usual topics, is conducted in an unusual way, and radically changes organizations. But it is planning and very detailed plans are generated. Boards understand about planning. Being asked to participate in planning is to be expected.

GETTING AT THE REAL ISSUES

As part of the planning process, have the board take an hour during a meeting and answer a detailed questionnaire, anonymously. It should cover not just the typical association goals and performance issues, but should address a wide range of drivers and include the issues that frequently plague boards and the effects of these issues on the association. If you use a standard questionnaire, tailor it to make sure the gut issues of your board are included.

Tabulate the results in a manner that allows the participants to see the answers by individual, though they don't know whom. They will soon recognize their own answers. This alone becomes a powerful lever for change.

Senior staff should answer the questionnaire too. If your association is large, all managers and supervisors should take it. The process you use for the board can work just as well internally.

First evaluate the responses (but read the comments last). Study the results until you can track each individual, at least on the board and senior staff, over the entire range of issues. Averages and chi-squares and other sophisticated measures don't matter here, individuals do. Your understanding of their motivations will make the difference. The usual automated survey reports seldom permit this.

Then mark each issue of consequence. We use a simple, understandable star system for this. We designate issues as being one *, two **, or three *** stars. Like fire alarms. Then lay out the plan of attack, which issue to deal with first, second, third.

Depending on the survey results, schedule a one or two day session with the board and the senior staff. Remove the tables from the room. Give no one anything to hide behind. We use an open ark of chairs facing large screens.

Harry's Story

Now it was time. That morning we had made a safe place and strengthened it issue after issue. Now it was time to face the first monster; there were three. The board had seen the price the association was paying for this monster, the pain it was causing, the hurts to the staff and (even) to me. They named the demon.

Everyone had known it all along, even Alice. All had spoken of it privately. But never had it been brought out into the open: George and Mike detested each other. Had for years.

It was time to ask the question. "What will you do about it?" The facilitator gently asked. He was looking from one to the other. No one spoke.

RESOLVING THE ISSUES

This does require some skill. If you know there is significant pathology or you want to save time, use an outside facilitator. Then begin, one issue at a time, bring their responses up, keep them before their eyes, and cause them to deal with them.

— What is the real answer here?
— What did we mean by this?
— What did this person (anonymous, but recognizable as an individual) mean?
— What are the consequences?
— What is the REAL answer?

Harry's Story

They both just sat there and looked at the screen, at the answers of their peers, even their own answers. Finally Mike said, "I'm willing to shake hands." George, red faced, curtly nodded.

The facilitator asked again, so gently, "Will that be enough?" The tension mounted still more. Again Mike spoke, "If it isn't, I'll resign."

"Me Too." said George.

The board nodded one by one, that would be agreeable. And then grinned and broke into applause. The energy was alive in the room and we knew where to invest it.

Don't let them hide. Hold the mirror. On the gut issues, they must talk about them emotionally. Intellect is never enough. Sooner or later on each issue they will say, "This is what we are, God help us." You are waiting for the "God Help Us." They have accepted, viscerally, what the issue really is. And let it go. Catharsis!

This is the point of change (on this issue). The energy that was tied up is now in the room.

You must move it immediately into a new vision. Ask, "What do we need/want? How can we phrase this?"

As they speak, record their words on the big screen. Sooner or later you will hear them say, "This is who we WILL be". You are waiting for the "WILL", their visceral commitment to the vision. Everyone will know it when it happens. Then you ask:

— What's the action?
— Who will do it?
— When will it be done?
— Who will follow up?
— Do you (by name) commit to doing this?

Then, and only then, is the energy invested in the future. Cathexis!

Harry's Story

Somehow, in our work, we had awakened the Association. It was again a living entity. It had made its needs and hopes known. It and we had found a new simplicity, a new vision. The energy released from all the politics and all the secrets had poured into the new.

The new looked a lot like the old, now the new was invested with commitment, power and the grace to motivate. Things long lost from the old. Irreversible action was already under-way with the promise to follow up and make it happen.

The process is gloriously simple and it works. It takes only the desire to do what is right and the knowledge that in the bright light of day politics are shamed and shrivel, dragons wither and die and secrets lose their power. Their power is released into the life of the organization and its future.

Harry X ——— is director of a not-for-profit organization. For obvious reasons, he wishes to remain anonymous.

The First Strategy of War

"The first strategy of war is a force that is fully mobilized and consumed with the desire to win. Without that, all other strategies are vain."

Napoleon

Today, we are all of us at war. For most it is a war of business rather than arms, but a war nevertheless, a real war. A struggle involving victory, survival, defeat, loss.

To succeed in war, we must learn the ways of war and master its strategies.

The first strategy of business war is a company mobilized and consumed with the desire to win.

There is a way for a CEO to generate the attributes within his company and managers that Napoleon so cherished in his armies and his officers.

The First Strategy of War

Today, we all are at war. It is a war of business rather than arms, but a war, a real war—of victory, survival, defeat, and loss.

The very environment in which we work teems with change; change that is greater and more rapid than we have ever seen in the history of business; change both in business and in society of a magnitude that in the past was driven only by the trauma and crisis of war.

This change comes from all sides and feeds upon itself, driven by technology, especially by that of the Internet and the web, driven by globalization, by NAFTA, by government regulation/deregulation, by economic fluctuation.

This lightening change is breeding chaos and crisis, disaster and opportunity for every business and industry; stripping market share and customers from the slow, destroying the concept of cost barriers, speeding the evolution of new competitive models, and breeding fear of becoming the next victim.

The need for urgent, aggressive and preemptive adaptation has become normal.

Companies of every size in every industry are struggling to make sense of this maelstrom, to conceive of ways that will provide for them a future, to instill and drive change not just through the corpus of their company, but through its very spirit. For just meeting the competition will not be enough. Soon, it seems, all companies must be either quick or dead. For we are at war.

To succeed in war, we must learn the ways of war, and master its strategies.

For the last fifty years or so, strategic planning has been portrayed as the single greatest tool of business survival and change and every business school graduate is taught it. So it is not surprising that so many managing officers and CEOs are turning to it.

But, in spite of all that is taught and all that is claimed for it, strategic planning has grave limitations. It is in this the war for survival that these limitations are proving fatal.

What strategic planning can do, we all know: it can provide some kind of direction, but not when the environment is changing rapidly; it can depict desired results; when done really well, it lays out step-by-step the actions that should be taken to achieve results.

What strategic planning does *not* do, has now become much more important:

- It does not mobilize.
- It does not ignite imagination.
- It does not trigger ambition or determination.
- It does not create or release the energy needed for war.
- It does not create flexibility in managers or agility in the company.
- It does not create the commitment or desire to win.

And, above all, when the resources for change are so needed, it does not generate profits.

Strategic planning is never associated with increased profits. A strange and disturbing fact that is rediscovered every five or so years. Even poor reengineering with its 30% success rate does better.

So what is a CEO to do? Is there a way to generate the attributes within companies and managers that Napoleon so cherished in his armies and his officers?

Fortunately, a process exists that CEOs and managing officers, even boards, can use. It is called Corporate Renewal, or Preemptive Turnaround, or Putting Fire to the Corporate Belly. It has been proven time after time in the spirit and on the bottom lines of companies large and small. Even in government!

At its simplest, the renewal process has just three components:

1. Uncovering and freeing the soul of the company. Bringing to the surface the real issues, the hidden issues, the secrets, and the demons of the organization. Depending on the level of readiness, these can be many or few, severe or mild. There may be strategic, financial or operational issues among them, but always they will have personalities and person-to-person relationships at their root.

2. Catharsis. Causing the management of the company to deal with the issues of the company until they are resolved. ALL the issues must be dealt with, but the core issues, the gut issues, the people and relationship issues must be dealt with first.

3. Commitment/Investment. Transferring the energies released into a gut commitment to a new future, a new behavior, a new flexibility and a new level of performance.

There are just two requirements for it to work:

- The managing officer must have self confidence; and
- The managing officer must have a deep desire to win.

Nothing else is needed. The process does the rest.

This all sounds easier said than done. How, for instance, do you get the senior managers to agree to do it in the first place? How do you get at the real issues? How do you do this without making mortal enemies? How do you take on friends of many years? How do you make them talk? Change?

But it *is* simple.

LET'S DO IT!

Not by chance, the renewal process is also a planning process. Granted, it is a planning process that addresses more than the usual topics, is conducted in an unusual way, and radically changes organizations. But it is planning and very detailed plans are generated. Managements understand about planning. Being asked to participate in planning is to be expected. Calling it Entrepreneurial Planning, though inadequate, would be accurate.

GETTING AT THE REAL ISSUES

As part of the planning process, have your managers and supervisors take an hour and answer a detailed questionnaire, anonymously. It should cover not just the typical goals and performance issues, but should address the fifty early warning signs of corporate trouble, the hundred drivers of performance, and the effects these are having on the company.

Tabulate the results in a manner that allows the participants to see the answers by individual, though they should not be able to identify who those individuals are (except by group) and should be able to recognize their own. This becomes a powerful lever for change.

Board members might answer the questionnaire too. The process you use for managers can work just as well for boards.

First evaluate the responses (but read the comments last). Study the results until you can track each individual, at least on your senior staff, over the entire range of issues. Averages and chi-squares and other sophisticated measures don't matter here, individuals do. Your understanding of their motivations will make the difference. The usual automated survey reports seldom permit this.

Mark each issue of consequence. We use a simple, understandable star system for this. We designate issues as being one *, two **, three *** stars. Think of them as fire alarms. Then lay out the plan of attack, which issue to deal with first, second, third.

Depending on the survey results, schedule a one or two day session with the management team; you, immediate reports and perhaps two or three more; maybe a dozen people in all. Remove the tables from the room. Give no one anything to hide behind. We use an open arc of chairs facing large screens.

RESOLVING THE ISSUES

This does require some skill and if you know there is significant pathology or you want to save time, use an outside catalyst. Begin. One issue at a time, bring their responses up, keep them before their eyes, and cause them to deal with them.

You ask:

- —What is the real answer here?
- —What did we mean by this?
- —What did this person (anonymous, but recognizable as an individual) mean?
- —What are the consequences?
- —What is the REAL answer?

Don't let them hide. Hold the mirror. On the gut issues they must talk about them emotionally. Intellect is never enough. Sooner or later on each issue they will say, "This is what we are, *God help us*." You are waiting for the God Help Us. They have accepted, viscerally, what the issue really is. And let it go.

This is Catharsis!

This is the point of change (on this issue). The energy that was tied up in this issue is now in the room. You must move it immediately into a new vision.

Ask:

—What do we need/want?
—How can we phrase this?

As they speak, record their words on the big screen. Sooner or later you will hear them say, "This is who we will be—so help us God". You are waiting for the *so help us God*, their visceral commitment to the vision. Everyone will know it when it happens. Then you ask:

—What's the action?
—Who will do it?
—When will it be done?
—Who will follow up?
—Do you (by name) commit to doing this?

Then, and only then, is the energy invested in and committed to the future. This is *Cathexis!*

The process is gloriously simple. And it works. It takes only the desire to do what is right and the knowledge that in the bright light of day politics are shamed and shrivel, demons wither and die, and secrets lose their power. And their power is released into the life of the organization and its future.

Then and only then, can the armies of the company be mobilized. Then and only then, can their commitment to victory be assured.

Then and only then, can the other strategies of business come into play.

Creating A Virtual Crisis

"Knowing what to do is easy. Making your people WANT to do it is the real challenge."

Dwight D. Eisenhower

Creating A Virtual Crisis
The Gentle Art of Provoking Change

In this time when change is the only constant, in this period when even the nature of change is changing and the pace of change is accelerating, when there is need for ever more rapid adaptation, when business is that which leads and drives the pace of change, humanity remains defiantly the same: reluctant to change; accepting of it only under duress; desiring to slow it to a standstill. In this environment, between the opposing forces of accelerating change and the human instinct for stasis, a CEO must exercise leadership. For without this leadership there will be no business.

It seems impossible, that this very real dilemma can be resolved. Perhaps short term it is understandable, in the face of crisis. But long term? Year after year? That seems impossible. Yet that is what is needed now. The skill of catalyzing change, of provoking change, of making people want to change, and do so time and again—without burning others out or being burned out.

"We're doing pretty good, really..." He had said it at least four times that hour. He was founder and CEO of his construction company. And they were doing well, at least well enough. But how could his staff recapture the enthusiasm they all had had fifteen years before, when they started this company on a shoestring, borrowing against a second mortgage on his home.

It was a situation we had seen many times before...

Our work is turnaround, business turnaround. But most of our clients are successful companies seeking surges in profits, or reversing the trajectory of their business or declaring new beginnings. Preemptive turnaround or early decline turnaround might be good descriptions of our work. But by whatever term, profit/performance improvement is what our clients expect.

In traditional turnaround work, the financial crisis provides management with the energy, the willingness, even the eagerness to change, to improve. In our work (upstream or devoid of a real crisis) we are faced constantly with complacency. "Lack of urgency" is the more polite term, but the real losses caused by complacency, measured in missed opportunities and business disasters bought for the future, deserve even stronger words.

Creating a radical improvement—in the face of complacency—is the very essence of what we do.

Some twenty years ago we created a process to break through this complacency and invest the energies and commitment of management into a new beginning, a new level of performance.

So, how can one do it? How can one learn? Fortunately, it is not too very difficult. Most of us have within us that skill, at least in nascent form. It can be understood. It can be evoked. It can be mastered.

ELEMENTS OF CRISIS

The concepts originated in our traditional turnaround work. We had observed, that in successful, crisis driven turnarounds, underneath all the technical and financial adjustments four events always occurred:

- A profound simplification of politics;
- A palpable discharge of emotional energy, corporate as well as personal—catharsis;

- An investment, and a deep commitment, of this same energy into a simple, clear, picture of the future of the company—cathexis;
- Immediate action!

So, can we contrive a crisis?

Of course! Sometimes your books will allow you to accelerate some write-offs and declare an emergency, announce retrenchment, get everyone's attention. (Beware: unless you own the company this can become an actual crisis for you.) But this crisis, now real, traumatizes everyone at all levels of the company—the innocent and the responsible. A huge amount of energy is generated by fear and lets loose destructively and mindlessly throughout the company. But some is left for you to work with at the senior levels. You can use it there to make the change you need; for all real change must come from the top.

This is not an economic way to do it. Nor is it ever safe. By far the better way is to create a Virtual Crisis. A crisis that is focused only upon those who must change and generate change in others.

THE VIRTUAL CRISIS DEFINED

Unlike a real crisis, a virtual crisis allows managers to energize and recreate a company. The keys to a successful staged crisis:

- It is based on truth (found through company survey).
- It is focused only on the management team.
- It is safe for all. (This is a guarantee the CEO must make.)
- It simplifies politics. (Once everything is in the open, there are no more secrets.)
- It generates as much energy as a genuine crisis for the people who experience it. (This must be experienced, but it is so.)
- It radically exposes the real performance drivers of the company to its managers.

- It forces true acceptance of what is—as well as under standing.
- It causes intense discharge of emotional energy. (This can get noisy, but that's OK.)
- It allows energy to be focused in a new direction, invested in a new vision. (The CEO must point the way.)
- It leads to immediate action. (The CEO must ask it, demand it if necessary.)

THE ANATOMY OF THE PROCESS

The first step is the creation of a virtual crisis. Virtual, because it is truly safe for both management and company. Crisis because it contains all the intensity of emotion that a real financial driven crisis would have and on which we can draw for the energy and commitment to simplify the politics.

The second step is to use the "crisis" to get management to identify and acknowledge the useless, dysfunctional and some-times pathological things that are going on within the company. And to feel, experience, express revulsion (catharsis).

The third, and this occurs simultaneously, is the investment of the energy released in the catharsis into a commitment, a deep visceral commitment, to a different way of behaving, of relating to each other, of doing business. A new blueprint: cathexis.

The fourth (again this happens simultaneously) is to create a detailed action plan to create the changes needed and commit, commit viscerally, to doing them.

All that remains is to begin immediately and Follow up! Follow up! Follow up! Of course, All of these steps hinge on the successful creation of the virtual crisis.

PREPARATION

To prepare for this so that everything else falls into place almost automatically, we use one of our questionnaires. The most frequently used is called "The Corporate 360°—Management Team Survey". It provides a detailed look at the organization, from within, through the eyes and from the perspective of the senior managers, the people most responsible for conditions as they are and who must lead and drive the changes that are needed.

The survey addresses (among other factors) some 100 drivers of corporate performance. These are the factors that actually cause, underlie, and impel the behaviors that generate performance. They are also the factors that cause complacency, that generate psychic pain in a company, that bleed the motivations of people to perform, to create, to succeed.

What are they, these performance drivers? The most obvious of course is morale, though that is not really important, more a symptom than a driver. Much more important are corporate (in)decisiveness, acknowledgment of work, communication of vision, integrity of management and relationships of managers.

CRISIS AND RESOLUTION

Once the management team has answered the survey, It is remarkably easy to create a Virtual Crisis. Management teams seem to know how to generate them themselves, with a little help from the CEO. There are just a few steps:

- First, create a safe, emotional place for your management team.
- Second, surface the real drivers of corporate performance. Work through the survey answers question by question.
- Third, cajole, force, insist and persist until the management team, individually and as a whole, address these at the emotional level and react, let loose, the energies of revulsion. (This is who we are, God Help Us!)
- Fourth, invest these energies in a new direction, a new vision.
- Fifth, take action.

A real business crisis creates havoc. Even companies that survive and flourish in the long term are weakened in the short term. Few can stand a second crisis in a single year.

But Virtual Crises, when done properly, are very different. They energize, refresh, and can be repeated in a quarter or so. Some CEOs who have really mastered the techniques can focus them, not only in the teams, but also on the issues and generate a process of continuous and proactive adaptation.

While mastery takes time, all that is needed to begin is a managing officer who really wants success and has the courage to make his managers look deep into the heart of the company and not flinch.

Inward Bound

When modest change is not enough, when competition or the economy or the world has become so different that a really new response is needed, then it is time for the company to change, to make a journey, to undertake a spirit quest.

Of necessity, the quest that causes lasting change must be inward. The greater the change that is needed, the deeper the quest must go, the more intense must be the search.

In the meeting of intense experience and business crisis we found a clue to something which a CEO can use, at will, to cause a performance transformation and a surge in profits.

The process itself is very simple. There are just three major steps, constantly repeated. Perfection is not needed and they become more effective with practice.

Inward Bound
A Journey of Corporate Renewal

When modest change is not enough, when competition or the market or the world has become so different that a really new response is needed, then it is time for the company itself to become different, radically different, so that its responses to the world in which it lives are different.

To cause a change of this dimension is neither an easy task nor an analytic one. It is not possible to buy or borrow or steal a strategy or a tactic or a system, however successful they may be for others. For such changes are but skin deep, transplants anyway, and are sloughed off by the company that is not ready for them, like foreign objects rejected by a human body.

To make a fundamental change in the corporate spirit, one that is really significant, it is necessary for the company to make a journey, a spirit quest. And the greater the change that is needed, the deeper in the quest must go, and the more extreme the experience the company must have to cause that change.

Many of us remember the change that happened within us in going through boot camp. It seems it should work for business teams as well. It certainly worked for the platoons we were part of. Boys becoming warriors and training groups becoming fighting units that trusted and could depend upon their men, and men upon each other.

For many years now, there has been much spoken of the positive change that happens to a management team that goes into the wilderness on an "extreme" experience—a kind of environmentally correct, boot camp surrogate with primitive traditions thrown in. Certainly it is an experience that few managers ever do forget. Just ask any participant.

Teams are formed, mountains climbed, rapids run, camaraderie established. Intense group loyalties ensue, at least for a while, and those who participate remember their experiences for years—often with nostalgia.

But few lasting business benefits are reported.

Some years ago, after sending a number of management groups on various out-of-doors experiences in the hope (certainty?) of creating teams who would create fundamental change within their companies, we began to question what was happening. The results were NOT appearing on the bottom-lines. (If they don't show there why do it?) The benefits of better teamwork, if any, evaporated in a week or even less. All too soon, the "teams" became again collections of harassed managers trying to survive.

It seems that training a team to play at football does not enable it to win at *baseball*. Neither does forming a team to climb a mountain or raft a river, train it to win at business.

However, there were a *few* reports that some of these trips had worked. So we asked the CEOs and managing officers about their experience and how that related to the bottom line results and measurable performance improvements they saw.

Almost immediately we realized the kind of experience they had undertaken seemed not to really matter. Rafting, climbing, trekking all seemed equal. The companies leading them seemed not to matter either. If the experiences were extreme, teams formed and could function to perform the tasks they were created for. But, for most, upon return to work, with the need no longer urgent, the task they were created for no longer there, the teams dissolved.

But a small few faced something different immediately upon their return—a crisis. A business crisis.

In these crises the teams, already formed, suddenly became functional task forces. They went to work without the inevitable need for gradual acceptance and emotional ramping-up. Crisis, business crisis, was the significant difference that gave results. Crisis caused the teams to function.

But crisis causes teams to form anyway. If not so quickly, or in time to do some good.

So! Is there something that a CEO can do—a real crisis being too dangerous a way to create a team and teach it teamwork?

There is!

In the meeting of extreme experience and business crisis we had found a clue to something which a CEO can use, at will, to cause a performance transformation or a surge in profits.

The program is called Preemptive Turnaround or, sometimes, Corporate Renewal. By both names it has been proven time after time since the early 1980's and it shows itself on the bottom lines of companies and in the way they compete.

In some ways it does resemble the out-of-doors extreme experience: it is intense—*extreme*, it turned out is not required. Teams are formed. Camaraderie is created. Challenges are faced and overcome, and team skills are developed. It has experiential features too. But the mountains climbed, the rapids run, the distance trekked are all within the company. The challenges overcome are those of the company and the demons conquered there are those that plague its soul. The joy, the exultation of achievement comes with a surge in profits. Those who participate remember. The teams do not dissolve come Monday.

Crisis without danger can be created when you know how. Let us call it a *virtual* crisis. And a virtual crisis can be used just as successfully as a financial one to create a team, a fighting task force, to change, transform a company and its bottom line. And that task force journeys inwards to the soul, to where the challenges really are, not outwards.

The process itself is very simple. There are just a few steps, constantly repeated. Perfection is not needed, and they become more effective with practice.

First, Create a crisis, a *virtual* crisis. This is the equivalent of the mountain or the river or the heroic trek, but it lies within your company. It should neither be hypothetical nor should it be expressed in financial terms. Lying is counterproductive and financial numbers motivate almost no one (however heretical this sounds). Early warning signs, the collateral expressions of corporate performance-like cash flow, are not much good either, it seems.

Select one of the drivers of performance and have the management team deal with it to full resolution. The drivers of performance are those elements within the operating dynamic of the company that cause behaviors that in turn generate performance. They are the attributes that trouble the soul of the company, and for which the senior managers are responsible, like morale, or integrity, or accountability, or acknowledgment of work and people. These are the factors that, if unhealthy, corrode the purpose, the energy, and the hope of workers. Refer to the Appendix for a list of Drivers of Performance.

Second, Visualize the company as a person. See it. Hear it. Feel it as an entity. Personify it. Give it form, shape and color within your mind. Identify its personality both as it is and as it should be. The more vividly you do this the more effective the other steps will be.

Third, Evoke the company. Call the management team together and force them to address the crisis you have declared. Do not let them shirk from this. Whenever the management team is making decisions for the business, the entity that is the company is there too. As you talk with the management team, remain aware that you talk with the company too. As you decide with them for the company's sake, you decide with it too. Saying to the group (and the company), "We are the company", is a powerful, empowering evocation. Also, whenever you talk to your workers about the company, which should be frequently, speak to the company through them and listen to the company through them.

Fourth, Have the management team, as a team, confront the issue selected. Ask them:

- —What is the reality here?
- —How do you really feel about this? (It's OK to get mad.)
- —What should it be instead?
- —What should I do, as CEO?
- —What should you do? Will you do it? When? When can I check?

Write the plan down, and enforce its fulfillment.

Issue by issue, as you do this you increase the power, the potency of the company to make known its needs, above the prejudices, the preferences, the needs of the individuals, above those of the CEO, if necessary. You are doing so by simplifying the politics of the company.

The simpler the politics and the clearer the focus, the more powerful becomes the spirit of the company. As the company grows in potency and in clarity, workers at all levels begin to respond to it as a separate entity. Creativity grows. Morale improves. The organization becomes more responsive to leadership. The key factors of the inner life of the company come into balance. External changes follow.

Repeatedly, over the last twenty years we have watched managing officers intuitively use these steps to turnaround companies and transform their performance. Frequently we have used these steps ourselves to enable companies to sharply increase their profits and renew themselves.

The steps may seem a little mystical, but they are as real as riding a bicycle. It will take you just a little time and effort to begin them properly. With practice they will become innate and the results will come faster. Once started, it takes no time from your day and the results of the normal course of business are magnified.

They happen within the heart and mind of the CEO. No one need ever know.

The Giving of Courage

The first and foremost duty of a leader is to give courage. Rudi Giuliani, Chief Executive of New York City, gave courage when it was sorely needed!

Investing in the courage of people brings extraordinary, even unwarranted, corporate results. In monetary terms it is free. The only cost is the will to do it. The remarkable thing is, you don't need to have courage yourself to create it.

The first step in this is to be there. Just be there.

The Giving of Courage:
The First Duty of the CEO

He was the Chief Executive. He had been in this position for several years. Many thought he had done well, better than his predecessor had for sure. Others thought otherwise. That is the lot of CEOs—not everyone will love them.

His personal life was a mess and many knew. Too many. He was finding it harder to muster support for things that needed doing. There was talk of his retirement. "Lame duck" was mentioned. Successors were discussed.

Nevertheless, on the day of crisis, in the time of trouble for his people, by instinct or by wisdom or by inspiration, he fulfilled the first and foremost duty of a leader—

He gave courage.

He did so quietly. He did so simply. He did so without pretense or bluster or grand rhetoric. His means were mostly silence. Just being there. Standing there before his people in witness.

He was their Chief Executive—he gave courage. Not just to his own people, but to the country, and perhaps the world. In that moment he was leader to us all. And all acclaimed him. All took courage and were stronger and with that courage could mobilize and focus and work again.

His name was Giuliani. Rudi Giuliani. Chief Executive of New York City.

He gave courage!

We men and women of business don't talk much of the needs we have for courage. It is not expected. It is not taught in B schools. We do not have the words. It is embarrassing since the absence of courage is seen as fear or at least anxiety.

But talk about it or not, we need courage. Our people need it. In the final analysis courage is what drives our businesses. It gives us the power we need go to work, to take risk, to create, and to thrive. Without courage we grow weak. Our people grow uncertain. They and we are fearful: find it hard to decide; find it hard to invest in our future; find it hard to communicate a vision of a prosperous future to clients so that they can invest through us.

I am not talking here of fierce, heroic courage needed in the face of great danger. The New York fire fighters and police showed that—in their lives, in their actions, in their deaths.

No, I am talking of a quieter kind of courage, an ordinary kind. The kind that let Giuliani stand silently and simply, there upon the devastation. The kind that let him represent us all and take symbolic responsibility for our future. The kind that let him become the focus of our fear, our anger, confusion, shock and then helped transmute these feelings into resolve.

Giuliani's was a quiet courage. A mundane courage, one might almost say. The kind of courage that could be shown on almost any occasion. But it was a courage so rare, it seems that when he showed it we were in awe of it and him.

>   We took courage.

Most of us, perhaps all of us, live our lives with feelings of uncertainty, of anxiety. It is part of the human condition. Our culture seems to cultivate it too and our educational systems seem designed to magnify it. Yet, for us to truly function, to succeed, as individuals or as groups, we must have courage; it is a prerequisite for success.

When we find a company where people exhibit courage, quiet courage, the courage to listen and speak, to argue, decide and thrust ahead, we find a successful company. We find the converse too, for failing, unsuccessful companies seem to breed timorous people. Or is it vice versa?

Courage breeds success. Success breeds courage. Someone must begin the process of giving courage and then sustain it. That is the duty of the leader. That is the first duty of the leader—no matter the title or position, CEO, COO, VP, manager, supervisor—

To give courage.

Giving courage is more, much more, than giving "encouragement." Encouragement, once a word of substance, has come to mean very little. Perhaps it is a kind of vanilla cheerleading. Perhaps it is an exhortation to do better. Perhaps it is a kind of verbal incenting, or worse, a sanction for failure.

En-Couragement means in its original sense, quite simply: the giving of courage to others; the instilling of courage in others; the creation or evocation of courage within others. A profoundly simple thing. A profoundly important thing. An incredibly rare thing too.

Who must we give courage to?

First, of course, we must give courage to our people. They need it from us. Just as we need and must take courage from our leaders, so our people need it and must take it from us. They can take it and multiply it if we give it. They expect it whether they know it or not, or whether they can articulate their need or not. If they do not get it, they will resent us for not providing it.

Secondly we must give courage to our peers, those who work with us, shoulder-to-shoulder and sometimes eyeball-to-eyeball. We must also give courage to our clients. They work shoulder-to-shoulder with us too.

Lastly, we must give it to our leaders. For sometimes our leaders are afraid. Giuliani gave great courage to his leaders.

How do we give courage?

It is no great mystery. It needs no special knowledge or cleverness or training. Just think of the best bosses you ever had and ask, "What did they do?"

What was it that Giuliani did? What did the mayor of NY City do that imparted so much courage to us all? In simple terms, there were just seven things, but all were acts of faith and generosity:

- First, he was there. He stood there to be seen, to be counted. That was the most important act of all.
- Second, he assumed the burden of responsibility, however guiltless he must have been.
- Third, he bore witness. He acknowledged the enormity of the injury and the challenge.
- Fourth, he showed emotion. Showed by voice and words and tears that he cared, that he felt.
- Fifth, he gave rich praise to those who labored.
- Sixth, he voiced certainty of success.
- Seventh, he spoke to his people as a people, as a single entity, recognizing their oneness and evoking their unity.

Most of us, thank God, will never face so great a challenge. Day-by-day, hour-by-hour, as managers, we have a need, a duty, to give courage to our people. So that they may grow in strength and hope and energy. We can do it just as Giuliani did.

- First, we can be there.

    For us, in our ordinary work, it means getting out and being where the challenges of our businesses are—in the plants with our workers; on the registers with our staff; before our clients with our sales staff; wherever the challenges and our people are.

- Second, we can take on the burden of responsibility.

    Even if it is the responsibility of someone else, taking responsibility is a defining act of leadership.

- Third, we can bear witness.

  Acknowledge the size and scope of the difficulties and the problems and the challenges to be overcome. Though they may be just the usual ones, they deserve to be acknowledged too.

- Fourth, we can show emotion.

  Show genuine, real emotion, human emotion—happiness, sadness, friendship, confidence, and worry. Business is driven not by cold logic, but by human motivation which is triggered only through the heart. If we are not demonstrative by nature, and many of us are not, then such little emotion as we can show will be seen as being all that we can do and appreciated all the more. Charisma is not really needed.

- Fifth, we can give praise to those who labor.

  Give honest praise, generous praise, public praise. Praise even though the work is not dangerous, even though the results are not remarkable. For work done day-by-day and every day is in itself heroic. It deserves praise—while the praised still live and can be heartened.

- Sixth, we can voice certainty of success.

  The need our people have for reassurance is at least as great as ours is, and ours is great.

- Lastly, we can speak to our people as a unit, as belonging to a single entity (not just one-on-one, though that is important too) and evoking that unity, recognizing the oneness of the group and its common cause.

  Rarely in our lives are we, as managers required to show great physical courage. Day-by-day, as managers, as chief executives of our companies, whatever their size, whatever their position within larger organizations, we have the duty to show the mundane kind of courage, the kind that Giuliani showed.

For that is our duty—to give courage. The kind that is unpretentious, open, honest and without shame. The kind that says: Here I stand, God help me; I take responsibility; I need help.

The kind that says: There is a future; there is hope; we will win.

APPENDIX I

The Early Warning Signs

The Early Warning Signs

NON RELATIVE

Acquisitions/Alliances
Benchmarking against
    competition
Budgets
Capital Adequacy
Cash Flow
Cash Flow Controls
Channel Stuffing
Collections
Commoditization of products
Controls
Cost Accounting
Costs
Cross Selling
Customer Retention
Customer Satisfaction
Dividends/Payouts
Economic Cycle Vulnerability
Executive Compensation
Facilities
Government Regulation/
    Legal Changes
Growth
Image
Incentive Programs
Industry
Innovation
Inventory Stuffing
Labor Relations
Legal Considerations
Management Visibility/
    Availability
Margins
Market Share
Organizational Redundancy
Ownership Involvement
Payables
Pilferage
Plans
Predictability of Performance
Pricing

Product Time-to-Market
Product Quality
Products/Services   (Currency of)
Profitability by division/company
Receivables
Sales
Sales Plans
Seasonality
Staff Performance
   Structure
   Technology
   Understanding of Financials
   Working Capital Availability

CHANGE MEASURES

Product quality (vs competition)
Product quality (internal)
New Products as % of sales
Sales force
Advertising
Promotion
Market share
ROI
Real Sales Growth
Capacity utilization
Value added per employee
Fixed assets/sales
Working capital/sales

COMPARISON with COMPETITORS

Quality
Prices
Costs per unit
Hourly wage rates
Marketing expenditures
Sales force expenditures
Media advertising expenditures
Sales promotion expenditures
Quality of customer service
Product image
Company reputation

APPENDIX II

The Drivers of Performance

The Drivers of Performance

Accountability
Achievement
Agility
Agreeableness
Assertiveness

Blame Fixing
Bureaucracy

Camaraderie
Change - Commitment to
Change - Eagerness for
Change - Initiation of
Change - Management of
Change - Pace of
Change - Resistance to
Change - Readiness for
Collegiality
Communications - Vertical
Communications - Lateral
Competition
Competitiveness - External
Competitiveness - Internal
Concern for Employees
Conflict Management
Consensus
Cooperation
Corporate Decisiveness
Corporate Potency
Corporate Risk Taking
Corporate Vitality
Creativity
Culture change
Customer Knowledge
Customer Orientation
Customer Quality/Desirability
Customer Service
CYA

Deadlines
Delegation
Direction of subordinates

Efficiency
Employment Security
Enthusiasm
Entrepreneurship
Excitement
Evaluation

Fear/Trepidation
Focus on bread and butter
Follow through
Frustration
Fun in Working

General Improvement programs
Generosity to other divisions
Goal Setting
Goals - commitment to
Growth

Image
Indices
  Adaptability
  Age Declining
  Age Growing
  Bureaucratic
  Entrepreneurial
  Sales Orientation
Initiative
Innovation - Focus on

Leadership
Listening
Long Term Profit Orientation

The Drivers of Performance (Continued)

Loyalty
of managers to staff
of managers to each other
of managers to company

Management
Visibility/availability
Development/Training
Commitment to Co.
Management Teams
Management Flexibility
Management Tolerance
Management Competence
Management Ambitions
Management Will
Marketing
Meetings - Conduct of
Morale
Motivation

Office Politics
Open Book Management
Operational Style

Performance Measurements
Performance Expectations
Planning
Praise
Proactiveness
Problem Fixing
Product/Service development
Profit orientation
Profit taking
Psychological Age

Quality

Recognition as Customers
*(parents/affiliates/other
divisions)*
Recruitment/Retention
Responsiveness
Risk Taking

Sales - Management Focus
Sales Efforts
Sales orientation
Sales/Customer Service Attitudes
Sense of Direction
Short Term Profit Orientation
Sr. Management Team
Stress
Success Drive
Success Momentum
Succession Planning
Survival vs Success Orientation

Trust

Understanding of What Others Do
Urgency
Vision - Buy-In to

Vision - Integrity of
Vision - Sharing of
Vision of Future

Willingness to Challenge/Suggest
Worker Involvement in Decisions

About the Author

Tom FitzGerald is president of FitzGerald Associates. He is a business catalyst and consulting management engineer. In practice for more than thirty years, he specializes in profit improvement, corporate renewal, preemptive and early decline turnaround.

He has worked with CEOs, COOs and managing officers of more than 200 organizations in the US, Canada and Europe, ranging in size from start-up to Fortune 500.

Mr. FitzGerald is also a writer and speaker. As a writer he is a frequent contributor to national and international business magazines. As raconteur he brings to vivid life the real experiences of his many clients as they transform and revitalize their companies.

By education, a physicist. By birth, Irish. By instinct and experience, a business catalyst. He is a long time resident of the Chicago area.

For more information about Tom FitzGerald's business practice, publications and keynote presentations, contact:

FitzGerald Associates
847-599-9960
info@managementconsultants.com
or visit
www.ManagementConsultants.com